The Truth, The Whole Shocking Truth And

Preface:-

I am Mitchell Spence, an ordinary person from an ordinary background, who, from a very young age had a dream, a dream that became reality through hard work and determination. I am not anyone famous, but I am and always will be, someone who puts others before himself and strives to protect and make a difference to other peoples' lives in a good way.

That is why I became a Police Officer with one of the largest Police Forces outside of London and this is my story, from the very beginning of that dream in 1978 aged just 11years until I left the service on 8th July, 2011, having been subjected to what can only be described as a campaign of harassment, oppression and ill doings by the 'organisation' just because I was an Honest Cop!

I hope that when you read this you can be inspired and realise:-

Anything is possible if you have the drive and determination to do it.

Fear is only something that gets in your way if you let it.

Standing up to be counted when something is wrong is a character trait to be proud of.

True strength is not a physical attribute, but something that is within us all and makes us what we are when it is brought out from within ourselves.

That there is a 'bigger picture' for our living and eventually dying, but we will never know the reason for this whilst we are still alive.

Family and those you hold dear to you are the most important things in life, not money, status or anything else other than good health because without those whom you love, what would your direction and life be?

The names of those involved have been changed and these names do not relate to any persons living or dead whom were so titled, but the accounts within this book are accurate and true.

Acknowledgements:-

I dedicate this book with love to my family, friends and colleagues who believed in me and who I am, for without their love and support, my future direction would have been so very different.

To those whom I have had the honour to share my experiences with and who gave me their support, of whom there are too many to name, I express my heartfelt love from deep within.

To those whom I have been wronged by throughout my professional life, I give them my forgiveness for the 'darkness' they showed and hope that, at some future time, they realise and reflect upon what they did and perhaps find the light to guide them to a 'better place'.

To my legal representative, Richard, I can never thank you enough for just being there when I needed you.

4

CHAPTER ONE-MY HISTORY.

I was born April 1967 into a humble family with my sister 6 years my elder and my brother 2 years my elder.

My father was a clerk and my mother was a housewife having previously been a telephone exchange operator and we lived in a small country village (which, at that time, it was) in the North of England.

As I grew up, we were a working class family who went on ordinary holidays to caravan parks in Wales for one week in the year and the closest I got to a holiday abroad was by watching 'wish you were here' or 'Holiday' on the black and white television in our lounge every Sunday, but we were happy and like every family, had our ups and downs and fallouts but never went hungry which was something my parents strived to ensure.

At the tender young age of 4, I had my first ever 'dealings' with the emergency services after riding my tricycle up and down the garden path until my foot slipped off the pedal and became trapped between the chain sprocket and the framework.

I was in tears and crying hysterically and so my dad asked a neighbour to ring 999 to get the Fire Brigade and Ambulance because he couldn't free my foot and was worried that I had damaged it. At that time, you were able to ring 999 without criticism and you would get the service you required very quickly.

In fact, not only did the Fire Service and Ambulance turn up at our address, but so did the Police.

That would never happen now for a call like that, but this was after all 1971 and not present day where 'performance targets' are more important than people.

I even made the local newspaper, aged only 4, with a picture of me sat on my tricycle after having been freed from chains (pardon the pun) and a story to go with it.

I always loved watching television programmes with my mum and dad on weekend nights so I suppose, looking back, there was something inside me from a very young age, perhaps even before 1978.

At 11 years of age I went to High School which was a major life experience for me because I now wore a uniform which made me 'belong' to something bigger and I was proud of that uniform because it was a feeling of 'growing up' going to a Comprehensive School and I always tried to be immaculate in my appearance.

To others, it was just another set of clothes that had to be worn, but to me it was deeper, some may think 'sad', but I was part of something that had 'purpose' and I was proud to wear it.

At that time, the School hosted a 'Police Week' whereby various departments from the Police came in and interacted with the school and pupils.

One of these 'interactions' was to show a film on a projector and screen because there was no such thing as a video or DVD recorder then, those things were still fictional things that you saw in popular science fiction dramas.

The film followed a Police Constable through one of his typical shifts and the 'jobs' he would deal with in those 8 hours of work.

That day, no, that moment after watching the film, was when I decided from deep within, that my future destiny was to become a Police

Officer and make a positive difference to other peoples' lives and NOTHING was going to send me off course with that.

I always remember the films ending, it went with the Constable saying "Now night shift, that's where the action is, I love working night shift" and then it showed him radioing in "sounds of breaking glass.......I'm going to investigate".

Ok, that was probably done for the film makers, however the Officer showing us the film then informed us that, after making the film, the Officer did in fact go onto his night shift one week later........AND WAS STABBED TO DEATH.

That never left my mind and in some peculiar way, made me more determined to join up, to finish what that brave Constable had started.

My time at Comprehensive School was not an easy one between 11years old and 13 because I wanted to 'keep myself clean' and not get into any trouble whatsoever because (looking back I was wrong in my thinking) I believed that if I got in trouble at school, then I would never be accepted into the Police and so I did have others bullying me, but who hasn't at some point and I was, after all, a target to challenge because I had always been tall and bullies are always small either physically or in their opinion of themselves.

That all changed at 13 years of age and I began to fight back because I had 'had enough'.

I must say that being 'good' for my first 2 to 3 years at Comprehensive School did give me the 'advantage' over others when I did my own version of 'conflict resolution' and was paraded in front of the Headmaster because he could not believe I would act in the ways that I did unless I was obviously provoked and so I received 'advice' whereas the other party I had fought with, was dealt with in a more severe way.

My 'conflict resolution' was to drag a lad into the toilets and put his head in the basin and flush it, as well as, in the middle of a physics lesson, go over to another lad who was 'goading me' and to punch him in the face knocking him off his stool and across the floor which made the girls in the class scream, oh, and I got a very, very long detention after school, but, I deserved that because I should have done this outside the classroom, not during a lesson.

I must stipulate, at this point, that I do not condone violence in any way whatsoever, but, self defence is something that must be accepted throughout, after all, a person will only defend themselves when they are attacked either verbally or physically.

There were other 'minor' incidents, but these faltered away after word got around that I was not someone who was going to take anything lying down and my time in Comprehensive School became much more quiet as I was 'left alone' by the bullies, in fact, I became somewhat of a 'peacekeeper' from then on because I would intervene in situations where other pupils were being bullied and the bullies would mostly back off, occasionally one or two would have to be shown the 'error of their ways' and it was sorted out to my satisfaction.

My vocation was decided, I believe, by 'powers' bigger than me and I had a 'reason' in life and a very worthwhile direction.

9

CHAPTER TWO – POLICE CADETS AND DEATHS DOOR.

To join the Police Force in 1983 you needed to have 4 'O' Levels or CSE equivalents and they needed to include English Language and Mathematics.

This showed that you were able to apply yourself to learning at a satisfactory level because there was and still is a vast legislative knowledge that is required to be a competent Police Officer and that is ever increasing in volume to this present day.

The required qualifications have now changed (although I personally think that that was a backward step) and 'assessment weekends' and 'assessment days' were introduced to choose potential candidates in the 90's.

So I left school with 5 'O' (ordinary) levels and 4 'C.S.E's' (Certificate of Secondary Education), something which I believe the current Government are looking to 'reintroduce' because the 'G.C.S.E's'(General Certificate of Education) have, in their own words, become 'too easy'.

I have recently read in the papers that the 'think tank' has now decided that would be recruits will, in the future, require 'A' levels or recognised equivalents to become Police Constables because of the complexity of the role.

Oh how the wheel goes full circle for this but it is a pity that the judicial system doesn't seem to follow suit in its sentencing.

The Official response is that heavy sentences just fill prisons and do not prevent crime, however ask yourselves this question, if a Burglar received the full sentence of 14 years or a Rapist 'life', then yes, the prisons would fill up, but, how many other 'potential' criminals would think twice about committing the crime if, when they were caught, they would know that they would serve the full sentence and none of this reducing same for guilty pleas or 'good behaviour'?

More prisons would have to be built and initially, the prison population would increase, but, after the initial influx of convicted criminals entering the prisons, the crime would decrease and the streets would become a safer place for honest law abiding citizens and their children to walk and live around.

O.k., the question of miscarriages of justice and wrongly convicted individuals must be addressed and the answer is simple.........in these days of D.N.A. and C.C.T.V. (closed circuit television) monitoring, the risk of a wrongly convicted individual going to prison would be questionable without a doubt.

In 1983, I became one of the last 32 paid uniformed Police Cadets ever to be recruited by the Police, much to my mothers' upset, because she did not wish me to become a Police Officer due to the recent Riots in Liverpool, Manchester and elsewhere in the country, as well as the animosity now within the Coal Mining Industry towards the 'Thatcher Government'. In actual fact, my mother had ripped up my original application form and so I had requested another and when I received it, I purposely left a photocopy of it completed in the house so that my mother would find, and, as I anticipated, would destroy it.........the original copy had already been sent off in the post by me the previous day.

I was originally resentful of her actions, but, with hindsight, I understand that her 'motherly protective instinct' played its part, very much like I would expect it to today when a son or daughter wishes to join the Armed Forces whilst there are conflicts still ongoing in Afghanistan, Iraq and other countries in the world where our Armed Forces are deployed.

No parent, as I am also, would want to see their sons or daughters enter into an occupation where they may well be in a life threatening situation, but, in the same respect, if their offspring are adults, then they should be allowed to make their own decisions and these decisions should always be respected, no matter how dangerous the resulting actions may be.

It is always better to support your loved ones and be a part of their lives where they come to you for advice, than to oppose them and resultantly, miss out on their future life experiences and the pride and pleasure that come from so sharing.

So here I was, a young boy aged 16 years now wearing a uniform that not only represented the Police, but also represented Her Majesty Queen Elizabeth the Second.

I will be the first to admit, myself and the other Cadets that I joined with, were nothing more than 'children' and still very much immature, so, to allow us to wear such a uniform was a major trusting action and some were, in the near future, to abuse that trust very disappointingly.

Out of the original Police Cadets, I believe that quite a few failed to progress through to complete their first two years as Police Constables, others having been arrested for offences such as Drink Driving, Theft, Taking a Vehicle Without Consent and some drug related offences.

I do not know what was going through their minds to cause this, but there was, at that time, a general opinion throughout some cadets and also regular Police Officers, that they were in some way 'untouchable' because they wore a uniform.

I believe, in my own opinion, that this could be put down to the Government of Lady Margaret Thatcher (the Iron Lady as she was referred to) because in the early Eighties, they needed the Police to be 'onside' with them because of the many strikes and disputes that were occurring up and down the country and so the Police were being 'awarded' regular pay rises (courtesy of the Sir Edmund Davies

Agreement) and confidence building comments from ' the Thatcher Government' and even personal visits by the then P.M. (Prime Minister) where they were 'policing' the N.U.M.(National Union of Miners) strikes and conflicts at the pit faces and 'Maggie' was utilising her 'spin doctors' to illustrate how 'hard on crime and disorder' her Conservative Government was.

This 'untouchable' belief was something I would come up against many years later when I was a Police Sergeant and also was fully qualified to be a Police Inspector; however that rank never became mine due to the latter opinions and corruption that I opposed which I will go into later in this book.

As a Cadet the next two years of my chosen 'career' would consist of two weeks on 'Divisional attachments' and two weeks training, both physical and legislative, although the latter was of little use to me and probably the others because we were not given the 'powers' that are available to you when you become a regular Police Constable and 'swear' allegiance to the Crown but that did not stop me from becoming part of a 'team' when on Division and I would always become involved in chasing offenders and restraining them with another Constable wherever I was needed.

Policing was so much different back in 1983-1985 and as a cadet, I was able to see many things, some which I have to say were not to my liking.

The television series' portrayed were very accurate reflections of the way Policing was back then and on several occasions I thought to myself "is this really how this should be done?" and "when I take my oath and swear allegiance to the Crown, I will do my utmost to 'make a difference' not only to the public BUT ALSO to the way the Police works in whatever way I possibly can".

I was 'attached' to the Lima Division which, compared to where the other cadets' were, was a 'quiet outpost', after all, what happened where I was?

It was referred to as a 'sleepy hollow' with sheep and very little else.

That description wasn't an accurate reflection because there was a major night life scene, of which, the majority was on one street, (the golden 400 yards!), where there were night clubs in abundance as well as bars and on the peripherals, some public houses.

Believe me, when the clubs closed at 2am, the Police were extremely busy, however, as a Cadet I was only permitted to work until 11pm, but I did witness some interesting situations with drunken revellers, (2am clubs closing.........that was the right closing time, not like now when some nightclubs are open until 4 and 5 am).

At 2am, the clubs would empty and the street was like it would be during the day in the Town Centre, a mass of bodies walking up or down, the only difference being that the majority were under the influence of alcohol, but, the Police were there and coped very well with any disorder that occurred.

Now the clubs are 'staggered' for closing and this, on paper, seems to be a better way, but, in reality, those leaving one club merely walk up to another if possible and so you end up still with many bodies up and down the Street and disorder occurring.

The only difference now is that the Police on duty are staggered on their shift patterns and you can see for yourselves that the 'thin blue line' has effectively 'snapped' because you would be lucky to see a Police Officer present when needed for these times.

Recent serious attacks have shown this to be a problem, despite door staff working in the bars and clubs (as at October 2012) and the Police Federation of England and Wales have stated in the media and on social networking sites that some areas have become 'no go' even for their staff after a certain hour.

As far as crime went, between 1983 and 1985, I can definitely say that the crimes I witnessed Constables reporting, were minor compared to later years, however the later years crime figures were certainly debateable of which you will understand further in.

I became extremely fit through my two years as a Police Cadet, the routines we had to do were aimed at that and our P.T. (physical training) Instructors had us running 7 miles up tall long hills and sprinting between lamp post lengths down to the bottom again, run uphill, sprint one lamp post to the next then jog, then sprint, then jog and so it went on, but this was the fastest way to improve stamina and really worked.

Gym sessions were also a 'killer' with 'burpees' (squatting like a frog then leaping into the air whilst 'star bursting' your arms and legs), then repeating the whole process again and again some 20 or 30 times as well as 'floor sessions' lying on your back with arms by your side then raising your legs together 6 inches, 12 inches, 18 inches, 2 feet, then opening them and holding, back to 18 inches opening and holding, 12 inches opening and holding etc, you get the picture?

These, together with many other 'pain' exercises, would see all of us change in our physical appearance for the better, some more athletic whilst others more stocky.

After these 'sessions' it was a quick shower and into the classroom for a 'law input' or onto the 'parade ground' for a half hour 'drill session' and inspection in our No. 1 uniforms, with the drill instructor who was incidentally, an ex Cold Stream Guard.

You can imagine what they were like bearing that in mind can't you?

Discipline was of the utmost importance in our training; after all, we were school kids who had now begun to wear a uniform representing Her Majesty the Queen.

Four months into my cadet role, my life was to take a dramatic turn...................I was at deaths door.

1984 is a year that I will never forget because that was the year that I should have died.

I had always been in the Scouting Movement, starting with Cubs, then Scouts and progressing into Venture Scouts and so there had always been some discipline within those movements and so, on one Friday in 1984, myself and a few of my mates were on our way home from Ventures, when an older 'friend' of ours offered us a lift in his fathers' Alfa Romeo 'Alfa sud' car.

He had recently passed his driving test first time and this was, unbeknown to me, one of the first times he had been 'entrusted' with 'dads' car and so we accepted the lift because it meant we could get our 'chippie supper' earlier and also down a couple of pints of one of my mates 'home brews' at his house. His 'home brew' was more like 80% liquor rather than 7% beer.

After collecting our supper, our ride home became somewhat scary because our 'older friend' decided to show us what his dads' car could do, much to my objections and most of the events that followed were 'blocked out' from my memory for many years to come and I could only remember demanding to be let out of the car, to which I was told "the doors there" which seems ok, but, when travelling at 60 mph around a corner, it is very much an impossibility, unless you have a 'death wish' which I did not and so had to 'hang on in there' literally.

My next recollection was being on my side, with my mate, who was of a rather large build, lying on top of me and the car window to my side being smashed and the road surface being next to my face.

We were on a road full of 'pot holes' and the driver had lost control of his dads car on a bend at 70mph, hit another vehicle causing the car we were in to career onto its side, MY SIDE, and then, despite that, continue along the road on its side, hitting another stationary car, causing that to move and hit another which then, in turn, hit yet another before the carnage ended and our vehicle, so I have been told by the Police at the time, eventually came to a halt.

At that time, the seat belt laws were not in place for rear passengers, of which I was one, and so I was very 'lucky' to survive for want of a better word.

I then passed out to be brought around again by adults reaching into the car, which was on its side, and trying to pull me out through the other window. As this was being done, the pain I felt was excruciating but I was unaware of what had happened to me then.

I passed out and became conscious again momentarily in a lounge of an address on a settee and was wondering where the hell I was and what the hell had happened to me. I was extremely lucky because the house I came around in, was that of a Nurse and she, God Bless her, was doing everything possible to minimise my pain and injuries that I had sustained........I believe to this day that her knowledge and actions saved my life that night yet I have been unable to ever trace her to thank her.

I spent the night in Accident and Emergency where my parents came to me and although I was in and out of consciousness, I will never forget the looks on their faces whilst at the foot of my bed.

My father did not speak, but kept looking at me, his face ashen with obvious grief on it. My mother just kept holding my leg and had tears in her eyes, but, each time I began to lapse out of consciousness, she would say, "Mitchell, DON'T GO TO SLEEP, WAKE UP......MITCHELL!"

Each time she said this, I would come around and look at her for this was something she used to say to me as a young child when we occasionally had a car that my father had been loaned from his work and we had gone for a drive out in the evenings. This was so that I would be awake to go to bed when we got home and I strongly believe that my subconscious related to this in hospital, subsequently rousing me again from what I thought was just a sleep.

I was trying to vomit and both my parents had been told by the Emergency doctor at that time, that I was purely suffering from shock and that the 'gagging' reflex was a direct result of this 'shock'.

In actual fact, at that time, my body was trying to vomit my intestines and contents of my bowels because I had sustained critical internal and bone injuries from the force of the impact, when the car stopped, my internal organs did not, thus major trauma injuries were sustained.

I was placed in the 'Intensive care unit' (re named 'high dependency unit' now I believe) and had a nurse by my side all night 'monitoring' me. I can talk a glass eye to sleep and that night was no exception, the nurse regularly telling me to get some rest, but I would not, why I do not know, but sleep was not becoming and how thankful I am for that.

You see, many years later, that same nurse became my daughters' health visitor after she was born and after many home visits, she realised that I was the young boy who would not go to sleep on her shift in Intensive Care.

It was then that she confided in my wife and I, something which, in her own words "had troubled her ever since".

After confirming many, many times with both of us that I was, in fact, healthy, she sat us down and opened up to us both. What she said was both shocking and upsetting for on that night in Intensive Care, she was instructed to 'note the time of my DEATH'.

I was not 'cost effective' and was going to be allowed to die with no medical intervention whatsoever because the Doctor on duty felt that my injuries would lead to my fatality sooner rather than later, but that was not to be for I was awake all night and destiny dictated that it was not my time to die.

The following morning, when it was ascertained that I had in fact, survived the night, more than eight hours, a decision was made to rush me to a 'Specialist Hospital' where I underwent a seven hour operation to save my life.

As a result of the accident, I had sustained a fractured pelvis, broken ribs, collapsed lung, fractured eye socket, torn bowel, ruptured spleen, my diaphragm had a half circumference tear and all my lower chest cavity had gone through that tear and was now in my upper chest cavity. I had also lost seven pints of blood to these injuries which was now also in my chest cavity from the internal bleeding and so only had two pints actually flowing around my veins.

So you see, I SHOULD HAVE BEEN DEAD, but for reasons unknown to me, I was not.

Whilst undergoing the life saving operation, for which I am eternally grateful to all the surgeons and hospital staff, I had my only Near Death Experience (NDE), which, until now, I have only shared with the few whom I felt 'needed to know'. These were friends and colleagues who had or were suffering bereavement and were struggling to cope, all of whom told me that my experience brought them great comfort and I hope, to those reading this who are or have suffered such loss, that my truthful account will bring to you some comfort.

NDE's have been described by some as 'out of body' floating above themselves, or deceased relatives being seen near to them or greeting them, or 'flying' high, well my own NDE was nothing like this, but is similar to other accounts, those where science tries to explain them away.

Obviously at this point, I was not conscious, but I was 'seeing' without use of my eyes, feeling immense warmth without any heat source, floating but without a body.

The only thing I could 'see' or 'sense' was a very bright light and being wrapped in total comforting warmth as if floating in a nil gravity perhaps which, as the bright light became more intense, so did the warmth and feeling of happiness in my entity, some may say soul, but as a sixteen year old boy, I did not understand what I was experiencing.

I only know that I WANTED TO GO TO THE LIGHT and it was coming closer and closer, engulfing me although I did not have any physical body here or eyes to see, yet I LONGED TO BE ONE WITH THIS BEAUTIFUL LIGHT AND WARMTH......and then my journey stopped and for a short while, I remained in this state of beauty, but then I began to withdraw from the euphoric experience, the light slowly, slowly moving back, the warmth ebbing away and I could do nothing whatsoever but 'see' it fading into the distance. I experienced emotional sadness at this because I wanted to be at one with whatever that euphoria had been and it was not to be, and that is when I felt the EXTREME PAIN in my physical body and believe me, IT HURT, IT REALLY HURT.

Who knows how long I had been unconscious, all I know is that my operation was seven hours long, but when I did eventually become conscious, I was faced with wires and tubes coming out of my body, machines monitoring my heart and lungs, a cradle over my pelvis to allow blankets on my bed without pressure and I was totally confused and distressed by the scene, so much so that I did in fact, try to remove tubes, but this is a common reaction apparently.

When my family came to my bedside, the first thing I told my mother was "Mum, I've had a most beautiful experience and I am not afraid to die!"

You can probably imagine my poor mothers' reaction to these words being said by her 16 year old boy, she broke down in tears and would not let go of my hand whatsoever, despite my having a 'drip' connected in the same.

When the surgeon was consulted about this reaction and what I said, he merely said to my parents "Your son was dying, what he experienced is not uncommon for those who are seriously injured, dying, but for him, it was not his time to go"

Many years later, when my dear mother passed away, I wrote a poem, which I can and I sincerely hope as you read it, so can you relate.

I called it 'The Passing'.

The physical body bears the pain,

When we all die, we're born again.

In death there is a happy time,

In celebrating this life of mine.

We all move on to somewhere new,

To tell those left, we cannot do.

For there is a purpose why we are here,

To care for those we hold most dear.

Now I have moved from here, this life,

I have no pressures, no troubles, or strife.

So long as you have memories to cherish,

My life, my soul will NEVER perish".

Whilst recovering in hospital, I felt very ill indeed, but whenever my family or friends came to visit me, I would always smile and joke with them so that I could try to minimise their worry despite, on many occasions, being in considerable pain as my body tried to repair itself and I could see their initial expressions when they came in to me and how they would pause for a couple of seconds to compose themselves before they entered my ward smiling.

I knew that it was extremely hard for them to see me in such a poorly state and I really appreciated their visits so I put on a brave face and when they had gone, spent many a night in tears.

My dearest sister did, I suspect, believe that I was 'putting on a brave front' because, after visiting had finished one evening, she came back to my bedside and asked me if I was truly alright, to which I told her I was because I did not want her worrying about me when she was not there.

That was a lie, but, for the wellbeing of those I loved, in my opinion, it was an acceptable 'white' lie, (Something said for good, not evil purposes).

I recall one young girl who was in the bed opposite me in Intensive Care at the Hospital (High Dependency Unit as it is now called), whose voice I shall never forget but whom I never had the opportunity to see face to face because all I could do was talk to her whilst on my back and, because of the positioning of the beds, all she could see was my big feet and so she called me 'big foot'(quite an accurate description really because I was a size 11 in shoes).

I never did get to see her despite my saying I would because, whilst I was still in recovery, I was told she had suffered a relapse and passed away.

May she be a beautiful Angel on High, rest in peace.

It was a long hard road to recovery for me, but I never lost sight of my goal in life, to become a Police Officer and make a difference and so I spent one month in a hospital bed, then, after learning to walk again (your muscles waste and your joints seize up through inactivity and constant lying down), I spent two months on crutches and then some considerable time in physiotherapy and I looked like I was a starvation victim, just skin and bone with a waist size of 26".

My recovery went well and I returned to the Police Cadets some six to eight months later. There is no doubt in my mind that my fitness was also a contributory factor in my being alive.

When I came back to work I made the decision to train to run a marathon and get sponsors and raise money to thank the hospital for saving my life and so I spent many more months running until I felt it was time to put it into action and I successfully completed the a local Marathon in 1985 in just over four hours and later presented the Hospital with a cheque for over £350.

I became known by Police on the Division as 'the runner' because, whenever there was a criminal being chased, if I was on hand, I would inevitably get involved and 'detain' the offender after a foot chase until the Constables arrived (a little later I might add!) but was never challenged because I was after all 6'4" tall and by now had more weight back on, so a force to be reckoned with somewhat.

I always kept my belief in good winning over evil and wanting to make a difference to peoples' lives.

In fact, I would stand in front of a bullet for what I believed in and did face a firearm later on in my career when I was a Sgt and my Constables were too afraid to intervene.

CHAPTER THREE – OCTOBER 1985 INITIAL TRAINING FOR CONSTABLE.

The 28th October, 1985 was the date when my dream became a reality and I was sworn in as a Police Constable and took the 'oath'.

Believe in your dreams and they will become a reality, after all, without dreams, man would still be primitive and my message here is simple but true......there are two paths for you to take in life and YOU choose which path you walk along, for good or for evil.

Only you can decide upon your future and if you can make your dreams come true.

I carried out my basic training in the City and then at a Training College where many Forces attended together.

The initial two weeks in the City were to 'show you the ropes' on pressing your uniform and 'bulling' your boots so that you had a 'mirror' finish to them which was and should still be extremely important because you NEVER get a second chance to make a first impression and looking the part can sometimes be the difference between 'sink or swim' in volatile situations.

My shirts would always be pressed and have creases in the arms and my trousers and tunic would always have 'knife edge' creases unlike some of the 'colleagues' that I worked with who looked like they had slept the night in theirs.

I always remember someone saying to me "If you look at a Swan, they are elegant and smart as they glide along the water or fly through the sky, but they are paddling like hell under the water and their take off and landings are clumsy".

Reading into that is simple, show on the outside that you are in control and you will be......nobody needs to see your nerves beforehand or your break down afterwards because the middle is all they focus on when they are suffering a trauma, no matter how small it seems to you, it is extremely large to them and that is so true.

After my first two weeks, I went to Training College and spent the next 14 weeks studying Law and all its complexities as well as going through intensive 'drill' procedures, physical training, lifesaving swimming and first aid.

Each week we had an exam on a Monday covering the last 7 days work and each month a 'stage' exam covering the last 4 weeks work, then at 12 weeks a 'final' exam.

If you failed your 'stage' exam twice or your 'final' exam, then it was 'curtains' for you and goodbye so you can see that the training then was intended to at least send you out with as much as possible to arm you for what you could experience on patrol and it didn't stop there either.

There was a 14 week attachment with a 'tutor' Constable on the streets, a 2 year probationary period where, if you weren't up to the chosen career, you would be asked to resign or be sacked and each month had a 'probationary training day' with your Divisional Training Sergeant where your knowledge of law and levels of fitness were tested to ensure you weren't letting yourself go.

In light of recent Government Reports, there is now an annual fitness test required to be taken by all Police Officers as of 2014 and should you fail this three times, you are dismissed!

In my opinion, this still does not go far enough because fitness whilst serving the Crown should be maintained to the maximum possible and I have worked with many 'colleagues' who, let's just say have carried a little too much weight to be efficient in the physical role they had, perhaps more suited to an annual appearance as a 'Father Christmas'.

If you put a comparison to this, how would our Armed Forces fare if they were not at the levels of fitness that they are made to be? It does not bear thinking about does it?

Why should the Police be any different? They could, after all, be the only thing between you and a violent criminal who wants to do you harm.

My experience of Training College wasn't a 'honeymoon' for want of a better word and, despite passing my 'weekly' exams with flying colours, I failed my first 'stage' exam and my story could have so easily ended there.

It was a 'wake up' call to say the least and I was subjected to the biggest lecture on failing not only myself but also my colleagues and home Force by my class Sergeants whilst paraded in my Number One best uniform as a 'disciplined' punishment.

I was terrified that all I had dreamt of was to be taken away and could not understand how I had failed such an important exam, after all, my routine was always as follows:-

Leave Training College on a Friday at 5.30pm on weekend leave,

Arrive home and have an early night to refresh my body,

Study all day on Saturday and learn all my previous weeks' law and procedure off by heart,

Test my knowledge with 'mock' exams all Sunday until 5pm,

Return to Training College by 7pm that Sunday and after a couple of pints in the residents bar, go to bed ready for the Monday exams, 'weekly' or 'stage'.

My 'wake up' call worked because, after failing my first 'stage' exam, I was determined that, over the next 4 weeks, I would NOT fail anymore and when examined at the next 'stage' on the previous 8 weeks, I WOULD PASS.......and I did, with flying colours.

It was such a relief and I remember, albeit distant and blurry, ringing home to tell my parents that I had passed, well......that's how it should have been, but after the relief of my results, I befriended my favourite tipple of 'Newcastle Brown Ale' with a 'Whiskey Chaser' and recall not so much my conversation with my parents, but more so the glass sections of the campus telephone box sides as I 'slid' down them whilst on the phone extremely intoxicated.

My mum and dad had to relay my drunken conversation to me when I left later that week on my next 'weekend leave', that is to say, once they had stopped laughing because they had never heard me so drunk but understood my 'binge' after so much pressure to pass.

Every Monday morning at 7am prompt, we were all subjected to a 'fun run'.

This involved being on the parade ground in your P.T. dress (physical training kit) and running non- stop for 30 minutes around the perimeter of the ground until instructed to reform in class ranks to be dismissed.

You then had to shower, change into track suits for breakfast by eight latest, to then be in full uniform for class lessons by 8.30am prompt.

Whoever thought of calling these periods 'fun runs' certainly had a warped sense of humour because there was certainly no fun in them whatsoever and these were repeated on the following Friday, after a Thursday night compulsory in the campus Bar.

Each class elected a leader and a drill 'pig' as they were then called and usually these were the ones who had left the Armed Forces (or services as they are politically correctly called now) and joined the Police and so you can imagine the discipline they would try to instil into us.

Our drill 'pig' was one ex Cold stream Guard and we nick named him 'awfully, awfully' because he believed he was a better class than ourselves and never shouted 'left, right' on drill, always 'deft, dight' because that was, he told us, the way the forces taught drill, well you can imagine the 'Mickey-taking' he got, but all in good faith and not malicious.

After a few nose to nose 'conflicts' with some of our class, myself included, he came back down off his pedestal and the harmonious balance was restored.

Training College was one tough cookie but necessary to ensure that the correct standard was achieved in recruits before letting us out onto the streets to patrol and any weak or unsuitable candidates were weaned out during that time.

After my basic training came the 'passing out' parade where your family and friends were invited on campus to watch you in all your glory show off your skills in marching and general drill displays accompanied by a fanfare with the 'chief Constables' or appointed deputies and one of the forces' brass bands playing music to accompany your display and was an extremely proud moment in my life, after all, if fate had been unkind to me, I would have been a mere memory and here I was, proudly showing my family that I had become a member of Her Majesties Police Force and I am sure they were so very proud to see how their youngest had turned out.

After the parade, you could take your family on a 'tour' of the campus before leaving through those dreaded gates for the last time.

The Training College was closed many years later, as were most of the other 'district training establishments' in favour of more 'on the job' training where new recruits, with little or no experience or training, would be on the streets as a group, with one or two fully qualified instructors showing them, in real time with real public, how to work.

In my opinion I DID NOT and still do not believe that this was anything more than a 'cost cutting' and 'public perception' exercise because you save money on overheads by closing the likes of Training Colleges down ('moth balled' for a few years in case problems arose and it had to be reopened) and you 'deceive' the general public into believing more officers are on the streets because they see numbers and not experience when they see a group of high visibility jackets on Police Officers.

The public would not know that out of each group of, for example, 15 officers, only 2 or 3 are fully qualified and efficient to carry out tasks required of them, the others are merely observers.

If a situation arose, then ordinary patrols from Division would be summonsed to deal and the 'artificial cops' would blend into the background again........how can that be progress and value for money for the public?

There is now a 'suggestion' or 'plan' to bring back the training establishments however all the District Training Centres or 'DTCs' as they were referred to have now been sold off and most, if not all, demolished so these will have to be new establishments at the expense of the taxpayer I presume. How the wheel is reinvented as a 'new' idea just amazes me.

The training period is also suggested to become six intensive weeks rather than fourteen as was the case before it all changed and my concerns are how can you have someone fully competent, fit, disciplined and adapted sufficiently to meet the demands of modern policing in such a short time?

My first major purchase as a Police Constable was my first motor car and proud of it I was too, however my choice could have been somewhat better.

I bought a Ford Fiesta......wait for it.......No, not an XR2 or XR2i which I could have chosen, but....a 'Poplar Plus 1.1.

Why a Poplar Plus 1.1 I do not know, especially as the cars to be seen in were the XR2 editions and as a Police Officer, in those early years, financial organisations would throw money at you to borrow so I could have afforded one, but I chose the Poplar Plus.

Don't get me wrong, it did me proud because after my wife and I decided to have children, that car was a 'Trojan' in so much as it brought my children home from the maternity hospital and never did me wrong, so it was a great car in that respect, but not so much a 'head turner'.

My 'children' are now fully fledged adults who have the right morals and beliefs and make me so proud to be their father every day of my life. So that was it, Training College was over for me and it was time to embrace the 'real world' of policing and I was to be posted to the Foxtrot Division as a Constable and what an eye opener that was to be.

CHAPTER FOUR - 'F' DIVISION.

At the time I was deployed here, inner city depravation was still at the forefront of peoples' minds and it was very evident in the area I policed.

I was the very first of the new recruits trained under the 'Police and Criminal Evidence Act' or P.A.C.E. as it was more commonly referred to.

This legislation was brought in to replace the 'old ways' of policing for the better, however, getting all the 'old school' Police Officers to agree with that was another matter.

They had Policed an era where an offender would be 'interviewed' without any formal records being made at the time and an Officer would or, should I say, 'should' have recorded something down into their pocket note books or on paper shortly after the 'interview' but this did not occur like that and, as a young cadet, I saw an officer 'writing up' an interview for court from memory because no record had been made anywhere and this was on the morning of the trial, months later.

When I asked about it I was told that it was as simple as this:-

"Did you do it?"

"Yes"

"Why?"

"Because I needed money!"

"Are you going to do it again?"

"No I'm sorry".

End of interview.

I did not know any different then because I was purely a young kid with a 'plastic' uniform and was a 'Y.T.S' (youth training scheme) as Cadets were described by many an 'old school' Police Officer, but, morally, and after training and instruction, you realised that that way of Policing Interviews was totally wrong.

Interviews and admissions were also made and concluded on the amount of 'fags' (cigarettes) that an offender would be given by an Officer (exactly like the 'life on mars' style in the television series), so that could not be the correct way to serve the public.

My first stations' relief (team) that I was on was shall we say, 'interesting'.

My Sgt was an alcoholic and his first words to me as he was about to drive off in a patrol car were "I'm your Sergeant and if I EVER catch you drinking on duty, I'll have your arse kicked so hard into the back of beyond, you'll wish you weren't born!"

He said this and then took a bottle of whiskey from his inside Police issue anorak and took several 'gulps' of it and then drove off.

I think you can imagine what thoughts were going through my head at that time.

That same Sergeant later in my career went off work on 'ill health' after failing to return in from a night shift in a Police patrol car causing all of us to look for him with our patrol Inspector 'on the quiet' for an hour or so before having no choice but to make his absence 'official' and disclosing it to higher ranks than he.

Within half an hour of disclosing, my old Sergeant drove back into the 'nick' (Police Station), to be confronted by my Inspector who gave him, rightly or wrongly, the option of reporting unfit for duty which he took immediately saying "Inspector, my back has been playing me up something chronic for some time now and so I am reporting unfit for duty".

In my opinion, he should have been breathalysed and, if shown to be over the limit, arrested and charged, but that was not my decision to take and despite making my feelings known to the Inspector at the time on a one to one basis, I was advised to 'move on' because no harm had been done.

My Inspector actually said to me that he understood my view and that it was the correct thing to do and, to my shock, actually admitted to me one to one, that he should have handled that situation differently, but that the Sgt was ' a good cop gone slightly off the rails'.

The relief was a mixed bunch of 'coppers', some long in tooth with 20 years experience and not wanting to 'embrace' the changes that were coming and some were between 4 to 8 years service and somewhat more amenable to the future of Policing, however, they were still 'influenced' by the older members and 'sang from the same song sheet' where required.

My role, I found in those early years, was extremely difficult because I was constantly being 'directed' by longer in service staff to carry out things differently to what should occur and I am glad to say, I REFUSED, but became subject to what would now be recognised as harassment.

The term 'sprog' was used to describe new recruits and the last one in was always the 'dogs body', "do this, do that, speak when spoken to or otherwise shut your mouth", that sort of thing and this came in 'waves' from certain Constables but I have to say, NEVER from my Inspector who was what I can only describe a Gentleman and genuine Police Officer.

I decided that I would tackle the 'sour' individuals head on if they chose to attack the new recruit and the changes that were being attempted to be brought in.

Constable Jayden decided that he would 'face off' with me in the locker room and try to intimidate me by threatening my career and, indirectly, my safety (if I did not 'sing their song' then when I needed 'back up'- calling for colleagues to attend your job if it seemed to be dangerous, or heaven forbid an 'assistance call'-where you are in imminent danger and need help a.s.a.p. would they come?)

I turned around to him and said "this 'sprog' bites back and BITES HARD taking no prisoners so do your worst, BUT, be ready for my reprisal because you will get that!"

Needless to say, he was out on a limb because, albeit some others were from the same era, none would go with him on his 'threat' and I actually got feedback from others that I had 'balls' to come back at him like that and so I gained a little 'respect' from them, (not that I wanted that type of respect from 'old school' coppers).

Constable Jayden even told me I could not park my personal car in the rear yard of the 'nick' until I had 'earned' that right so I made every effort to do just that, on one occasion coming back in from foot patrol to find that my car had been blocked in by several patrol vehicles (I suspect all moved in place by him) to prevent my travelling home until the next shift turned out.

The following shift were very obliging in moving the vehicles for me because at that time I was not a qualified police driver and so to do so myself would have amounted not only to a discipline offence, but also a criminal one of taking a vehicle without consent (T.W.O.C) or (U.T.M.V), unauthorised taking of a motor vehicle.

When my next duty came, I dealt with his actions immediately by attending early and making his uniform into a state of disarray without damaging anything. This I did by tying all his sleeves in his jackets into very tight knots, creasing (well to be accurate, adding to his creases already there) his shirts and, removing without breaking, his helmet badge and placing it back upside down as well as handcuffing his belt to his trousers with his issue hand cuffs and filling all his pockets with the 'waste' from the office equipment hole punch (the instruments used to put equal holes in paper to place in a ring binder) just as a little statement to back up my answer to his 'threat'.

It took him some considerable time and he vented some considerable frustration whilst trying to sort his 'problems' out which also made him late for the 'parade'(where the Sergeant goes through all the crimes since last on duty and allocates your beat to work and other matters) and so he had some explaining to do for that.

He did challenge me in front of the 'relief' and my answer was simple "THIS sprog bites back"!

I gained a large amount of respect for my actions that day and he was somewhat a 'laughing stock', but needless to say, he never tried anything like that again!

I believe 'Karma' is a real occurrence, if you do good, then good comes to you, BUT, if you do bad, then bad things will come to you and in Constable Jayden's case, his 'Karma was, in addition to the immediate actions that I took, later on in his career, after I had been promoted to Sgt (Sergeant), he transferred to my Division and had to 'request' my permission to return from patrol and enter the 'nick' (this was because that was how it was done in the city but not on the Lima Division), however, I omitted to let him know this and so for several months this is what he would do and I would ask him for his reasons for the request over the air, much to the amusements of his new found colleagues who were 'in' on this little game of mine, after all, he had become the 'new sprog' (in his own historic terminology) on the Division and had become a 'small fish' in a big pond.

Another colleague of mine on the Foxtrot Division was known by the nickname of 'Emu'.

Such an unusual nickname and I wondered if it was because he would 'bury his head in the sand' if trouble came or wrongs were being done but I am glad to say this was not the case. Constable Anders as I shall refer to him , 'earned' the nickname because he was in pursuit of a stolen motorcycle once and this motorcycle went across a school field, hotly pursued by Constable Anders (yes across a school field in a mini metro.....remember those tiny things?)

Well yes, they had become Police patrol cars and what a mistake that was.

Anyway, as the motorcyclist went across the field, there was a deep contour (change in height of the land) which meant a deep drop but the motorcycle could 'jump' this without much problem, the mini metro however, could not!

I did not witness this fete, however, from what I was told, it would have put the 'Dukes of Hazard' and Eddie 'The Eagle' Edwards to shame because the 'Emu' took to flight, well sort of, and the car landed in somewhat a state of disarray, oh and plenty of damage to go with that, hence the name 'Emu' because we all know an Emu CAN'T FLY.

Constable Anders was an extremely polite and honest copper, one of those I referred to earlier and had approximately 6 years in when I joined whom I still have great respect for now.

Constable 'Awky' as I shall refer to him, because that was his nickname, was, at that time, in 1986, a somewhat 'opinionated' character whom you would not wish to get on the wrong side of, however, later on in service, I came across him again and the change in his character, outlook and demeanour was amazing, I could not believe it was the same person I had previously worked with when I was a probationary Constable.

I was placed with 'Awky' who at that time was a local area bobby (Neighbourhood Policeman as they are now called) for a period of two weeks to gain an insight into how they Policed the local community.......wow, what an insight that was because he had earned the 'respect' (or more like fear) of his community by the way he dealt with individuals on his beat.

He would walk along his 'beat' with his helmet off, tie off and smoking a rollie, a self rolled cigarette, (ties then were only allowed off if the Chief

Constable gave authority on Force Orders and only in hot weather and obviously smoking anything whatsoever whilst walking foot patrol was a big NO).

Helmets, well that was self explanatory, if you're on foot patrol, you wear it.

None of this bothered 'Awky' and sometimes it was like walking with a wild- west bad boy because, when he walked along and saw certain criminals outside their houses, they would literally get inside quickly and close the door.

From what I gathered, Constable 'Awky' Policed with his fists and weight because he wasn't exactly a small build to say the least.

I always remember when I made the mistake, and it was a mistake, to find out why his nickname was 'Awky'.

We were walking along a virtual empty road on his 'patch' (beat) because the individuals who saw him had retreated into their houses and I asked "why do they call you Awky?"

Constable 'Awky' immediately stopped dead in his tracks, put his hands on his hips and roared laughing, to finish off with "Why do they call me Awky, WHY DO THEY FUCKING CALL ME AWKY?" followed by shouting extremely loudly "BECAUSE I'M FUCKING PIG AWKWARD AND IF THEY DON'T KNOW THEN THEY FUCKING WELL WILL DO SOON ENOUGH".

I have to admit it, he was a somewhat 'imposing' character and I was the new kid on the block, the 'sprog' and by God, I felt so small at that moment in time.

My 'tutor constable' whom I worked 'in company' with (being taught to be a competent officer) was Constable Jameson and he was a very young professional officer who taught me well and I could relate to him like a big brother.

Constable Jameson had the same morals and ethics as I to 'protect truth and Justice but fight corruption and lies' and he, on several occasions, brought my 'relief' (working colleagues) around to the correct way of thinking, after all, he had been on the relief for several years when I came and had embraced change with an 'open mind', accepting that change took place for a reason and the 'old ways' had to go to be replaced by new for the better of all concerned.

Another of my relief was Constable Samuels and he was 'old school' in many ways however his heart was, most of the time, in the right place, but he did see himself much like the character out of the American film 'choirboys' (about an American Police precinct in N.Y. New York).

Constable Samuels would refer to most, if not all of the known criminals as 'chicken shit' and always to the local Station as 'L.H.P.D.' ('P.D.' referring to Police Department).

I was on patrol with Constable Samuels who took me 'under his wing' once my 12 weeks of 'tutoring' had finished and drove me around on night shift in a battered old Vauxhall Chevette Police car which had no blue lights on and that was 'his' car because he could 'sneak up' on criminals because they did not realise it was a Police car until it was upon them.

I always remember that Police car because, at that time, vehicles were only replaced if they had to be and on one rainy night, Constable Samuels was pursuing (chasing) a criminals car and as we went over a large mass of water on the road, I got drenched because the foot well had A HOLE in it, yes, A HOLE and as we went over the water, it was like a fountain coming up at me.

Constable Samuels had not told me about the foot well and I had not seen it so I got very wet inside a police car.

He could not stop laughing and told me I had just been 'baptised' into the 'L.H.P.D. way of life and the rest of the relief shared his joke because many of the younger in service officers had also been 'baptised' in a like manner!

Constable Samuels referred to me as his 'law book' because, in his own words, he was "too long in the tooth to change his ways".

One day, whilst on patrol with Constable Samuels, we had occasion to attend an address where an offender whom he had been after for some time resided.

I was asked by him what his powers to enter to arrest this male were and the law stated that "if a person is suspected of committing an 'Arrestable Offence' (one that was specified as such or for which, on conviction, a sentence of 5 years or more could be given) and you (the Constable) have 'reasonable grounds' to suspect that that offender is inside the premises, then you may use 'reasonable force' to enter and effect that arrest".

Simple to understand and action, however, at that moment in time, Constable Samuels did NOT have reasonable grounds to suspect that the offender was present, this was merely his last known address and so, as I started to recite the 'powers' available to him, I had got no further than answering "YES, IF....." and that was it, the door had been kicked in by Constable Samuels and he was inside much to my shock and horror.

I could do no more than to follow him inside because he was now 'at risk' of assault, however, I was still covered by the law because it was Constable Samuels whom had used Force and not I and my purpose was to 'protect life and property', be it that of Constable Samuels or that of the suspect.

As I entered the first room, out came Constable Samuels with his suspect held by his EAR, which was something I looked at in amazement because his 'suspect' was a grown ADULT, obviously fearful of him and what may happen if he did not comply.

This was the 'Policing' that the locals had become used to, and perhaps the rest of the country under the 'Thatcher Government', HOWEVER, it was WRONG and I was one of those 'new breed' whose role it was to show them the correct way to behave and Police.

Being a Police Officer in a deprived inner city area was not an easy thing to deal with for a spouse and my wife was no exception to that, however she was, I knew, the only person whom I loved with all my heart and soul and whenever I went to work, I would kiss her last and tell her tenderly that "your kiss is the last thing on my lips before I go to work".

In those days, a Police Officer being killed on duty was still a rarity, but it was always in the back of your mind that one day may be your last and at this point I want to remember ALL the Police Officers whom have paid the 'Ultimate Sacrifice' as unarmed 'protectors', for they are all citizens who chose their career and direction in life to 'make a difference' and swore allegiance to the crown and citizens of our beloved country, most recently the two Female Police Constables who were 'butchered' and taken away from their families and friends in such an awful, cowardly way (September 2012).

I wrote this poem in their memory:-

God has chosen to take you now,

We don't know why, but we do know how.

Your lives were short,

But you were so very brave,

No more with the trials of life,

You will have to slave.

You both wore your badge with the utmost pride,

You were called to your deaths by an Evil man who had lied!

So young, so much of your life still ahead,

But now, in this world, your bodies are dead.

Rise up into Heaven,

Your work here is done,

For Eternity now, with your God you are one.

When I first met my wife, I told her within 2 weeks that I loved her and I knew in my heart that she was my 'soul mate' with whom I would spend the rest of my life.

Despite her telling me "You cannot love someone so soon", I knew that she was the lady whom I had been searching for and, unless something beyond my control occurred, I would do everything within my power to make her mine and would cherish every moment with her for that lady would make my life whole.

I could never put myself in her shoes because I could not cope with reversed circumstances and letting her go on duty in a city at night, I just do not know how she coped with that and the fact that she was a civilian and nothing to do with the Police whatsoever illustrates just what a strong person she was because, if she was ever worried about my career, she never showed it, BUT, she was ALWAYS there for me, as were my children, now adults, later in life, through some seriously dark days in my career and for that I can NEVER thank them enough.

Night shift in was always interesting and I would always make a point of walking down the back alleyways checking doors and windows and listening, just listening for the inevitable alarm activation or glass smashing, that sort of thing and I was never disappointed.

My view was that you did not see things happening in street lighting or on main roads, you had to be in the shadows, lurking and waiting and this I did despite being 'pulled up' by a Sgt warning me that if you did that, you could end up dead.

Despite that, I always believed in 'a good days work for a good days pay' and nothing else would alter that view.

That attitude would lead me into some considerable action, some good and some not so, but I was paid to do my job and do it well and so that is what I did.

Our uniforms had been changed 'for the better' (out with the old practical anorak and in with the 'storm coat' – anorak waterproof, storm coat wet......wetter than anything in rain, in fact you might as well have jumped into a lake and you would have come out dryer! Out with the warm dry cleanable trousers and in with the new 'better' washable lightweight trousers that would mark if you pressed them too hard).

No more warm, dry walks on my beat now.

Anyway, my 'storm coat'.......... well, at the time all we relied upon for our self defence was a 12" stick of wood referred to as a 'staff' or 'truncheon' (female officers had been issued with a 6" stick of wood which was as practical and helpful as a 'chocolate fireguard') and this fitted in a specially designed pocket on your trousers (a truncheon pocket as it was known) (female officers carried theirs' in the issue handbag until they were both recalled – one change for the better at least) and I always had the leather strap of my staff hanging out from the pocket so that it was easily accessed and our 'old' anoraks were just short enough to allow you to grab the staff if needed.

The new, 'better' 'storm coat' however, was not and completely covered your staff pocket because the coat went down to your knees, very practical, not.

There was, however, an inner pocket that you could reach through to grab at your staff and, in theory, withdraw it effectively, through your storm coat and into 'play' should circumstances deem this necessary. This did not work and many a Constable was seen rummaging in his pocket trying to bring out their staff which looked a little peculiar to say the least.

My wife came up with an excellent idea to counter the impracticality of the storm coat and access to the 'staff' which we should have 'patented' really because it was simple but effective, however, the uniforms then and up to when I retired in July 2011, were all short lived and replaced with new, more practical (whatever) better uniforms.

The amount of wasted tax payers money over the years is scary and yet I do not think it will stop because there is always some 'think tank' on the go changing things or 'repairing' something that isn't broken merely to justify their existence.

I have seen only recently in January 2013 that the body armour seems to have now changed again and it is a black material with netting on as opposed to blue when I retired so you can see, it still continues now.

The idea was simple, we cut off the top of the issue tie just below the false knot (because all neck ties were clipped on so that if someone tried to grab you by it, the tie would just fall away – however, with some of my ex 'colleagues' you would not be judged if you thought it was because they COULDN'T fasten a tie).

The lower part of the tie was then stitched, upside down, into the inner side of my storm coat near the lapel, and, once securely stitched in, I could place my staff into the adapted tie and have the wrist strap at chest level, to grab if needed immediately.

Very clever indeed, but, it has to be said, it was my wife who adapted it and I merely wore it with pride and satisfaction because it would not be long before I utilised this 'fast release' staff.

One night, whilst on foot patrol on a Town Centre, I checked a central alley way from which all the main shops connected.

It was pitch black and I would always pause for a minute after entering to let my eyes adjust to the darkness and listen, just listen, before proceeding along the building lines checking the doors and windows.

In the dead of night and pitch black, your senses must enhance to allow you more 'warning' of things not being right and so your mouth goes dry, your pupils dilate, your breathing shallows and you 'tip-toe' around slowly and if you had any sense, like me, you would buy a cheap ear piece for a transistor radio and plug that into your P.R. (Personal Radio) so that you had the advantage over any criminals.

In 2012, the 'airwaves' personal radios are equipped with an earpiece to ensure privacy in information received but the original 'Burndept' three channel radios of the eighties were not.

I would always wear a lightweight scarf, black in colour too, so that my shirt and collar could not be seen and would use black non permanent felt tip pen to cover my helmet badge and any buttons that may be on show when carrying out night foot patrol because the slightest 'glint' of light could give me away and I wanted a 'stealth' approach always.

Now this alley way was nothing special, I had checked it at least twice each night and knew it off heart like the back of my hand, in fact I could have been blind-folded and taken anyone through it because I had checked it so many times in the pitch black, the dead of night, until...........THIS NIGHT!

One business had taken it upon themselves to install motion sensors connected to two very powerful spot-lights and had not forewarned the

Police (not that they had to, but it would have meant a few less grey hairs appearing on my head).

So, picture this, here I am, slowly and tentatively minding my own business, checking the rear doors in this pitch black alley way, having put all my senses into a heightened state, when all of a sudden I hit the sensors range and BOOM, the whole alley is lit up with blinding light as if a U.F.O. (Unidentified Flying Object) had just put on its main beam over and around me ready to take me away!

For several seconds I could not see a damn thing, my pupils were now totally dazed and I had no idea what was happening, where this light was coming from and so, instinctively, I reached for my staff in its new 'quick release' home and drew it with such speed and force if it had hit anyone, It would have done serious damage.

I spun that staff around my head and body so bloody fast as I retreated I must have looked like a 'Tasmanian Devil' out of one of the Warner Brothers cartoons, 'NINJA MITCH' was in action and I only stopped when I realised what a fool I was and what had actually occurred, silly me.

From that night onwards, my patrolling of that alley way was made so much easier by those sensor lights because It was like daylight when they were on and I could check all the doors and windows in half the time, until, one night, I strolled into the alley way readily expecting the lights to come on as I got to a certain point, but they did not!

So now, it was back to the 'old school' way of checking this night, but with the added adrenalin caused by the knowledge that they should have come on, but they did not, why not?

Many, many thoughts were going through my head, first and foremost was the fact that I have confidently gone beyond my safety zone by walking in, without my staff or torch ready fully expecting there to be light and so now I am half way down an alley, not knowing if anyone is in front lurking, or behind and that really does make your skin creep.

After adjusting to the blackness, I began to check the property slowly and meticulously, staff in my right hand and doors and windows checked with my left, I was taking no chances whatsoever.

Windows, doors and handles checked and so far, so good, until...........

The next door handle I tried, turned and pushed was locked, but the whole door and frame had been removed from the fixings and so, as I turned the handle and pushed the door, which was an old heavy wooden type on an old building, the whole unit fell in and onto the floor, with my hand and the rest of me still attached, now also flat on the floor and extremely vulnerable to attack.

After hitting the deck, (the floor and very ungraciously too), I became more aware of my vulnerability if burglars were in fact inside and so out came the 'ninja' again!

Spinning my staff around I got myself to my feet and immediately called for 'back up' (requesting other officers to attend the scene to help me) and I then began my search of the premises slowly and meticulously.

The air was still, the silence was deafening, my heart was pounding and my adrenalin was through the roof. You've heard the expression when it is said 'the hairs on your neck rose', well that is so true and this was my very first experience of it.

The burglars had even cut off the power supply and so it was my eyes and ears that were working to their limit now. Each room I checked, my right arm with staff in it raised to my side ready to hit anything that moved.

I would 'take them down' before they did the same to me, that was sure and then I heard what I really did not want to hear, sounds of movement from further inside, a small 'thud'!

As I approached the stairwell, the noise came again, from upstairs, where was my back up when I needed it?

Still alone, I slowly ascended the stairs in total darkness, breathing faster and faster but shallow and trying to be calm but human nature kicks in and there is another saying, 'adrenalin is brown', well I didn't want to find out if that really was true!

Onto the landing of the first floor I went and heard an almighty smash from my right.

I jumped back totally startled and somewhat in the grips of fear (well I was, after all only 19 years of age and in a violent area in the middle of the night on my own in total darkness and experiencing my very first burglary not knowing if other officers were on their way to me or not and I had sworn an oath to 'prevent and detect crime and bring offenders to justice).

This was real and yet 'surreal' too and in the back of my mind was the thoughts of my family and that I was not 'superhuman' and merely a mortal who could be killed, but this was the direction in life that I had chosen ,or had it chosen me?

After taking a few breaths to calm me down I knew that I had to go into the room where the noise had originated.

As I entered the room, I slammed the door back only to be attacked..........by a cat!

The damn thing jumped straight at me screeching and bloody hell, I swung my staff around as it jumped at me and scurried off and away. I must have caught it when I slammed the door open to gain the element of surprise which caused it to screech and come straight for me and to this day, I don't know who was more petrified, me or the cat?

A bloody cat inside a building, I wondered how and then why before catching my breath again, laughing to myself and then carrying on with the job in hand, to secure the rest of the premises, which, at that time, had completely gone from my head, but the fact was, burglars could still be inside and could have a weapon.

It seemed like ages, but after checking all the rooms, I was happy it was empty and the crime had already been completed prior to my discovering it and then, after I had done my duty on my own, my 'back up' arrived!

Well, I still had another six hours to do on my tour of duty that night and so my beat would continue to be patrolled by me after securing the property and reporting the crime.

In those days, crimes were reported as they were and very rarely 'edited' or 'reclassified' to assist 'statistics' as they are now which I personally feel is a form of corruption in itself because if a victim reports a crime, then unless it can be shown to be false, it should remain a crime as reported, but I have witnessed and fought against, so many crimes that were 'downgraded' by 'bosses' to make the detection rates better and figures more 'suitable'.

The remainder of my tour of duty that night was uneventful, but I kept my experience of my very first 'cat burglar' to myself for the rest of my career, until now!

Night patrol was difficult because your body is 'designed' to sleep, recharge and repair itself at night and yet you were unnaturally forcing yourself to go against all your bio rhythms, sleeping in the daytime and awake at night and no matter how much sleep you had had, you were always sleepy on nights.

The mortality rate (age after retirement before you died) in the Police when I first joined was fifteen years so you can imagine how that felt knowing that 'statistically' I could be dead at the age of sixty three and a half years of age when I would have done thirty years service to forty eight and a half, then fifteen years of 'life' before potential death.

In 2012, the mortality rate was allegedly six years after retirement.

I was determined that I would prove the figure makers wrong, however, throughout my career, I was reading about retired 'colleagues' on the

'Chief Constables' Orders' whom had died and it seemed that the figure makers were very accurate indeed, which was a 'sobering' thought.

There was a general pattern emerging with the police in so much as the 'earlier' 'Dixon of Dock Green' style 'bobbies' whom had joined up in the late fifties and early sixties, were living to ripe old ages of seventy or eighty but, sadly, the bobbies that joined after that time, in the late seventies and eighties, were dying quite young (young as in within ten or fifteen years of retiring) and I strongly believe that this had a lot to do with the pressures that were being placed upon police officers from that time up to present day (in fact up to when I retired on ill health because of major 'dark' influences which I fought against).

I had seen the legislation change immensely, powers of Officers made much more difficult to apply, tours of duty becoming much longer, demands to work cancelled 'rest days'(days off for you to recuperate) increase, a 'blame culture' emerge from the 'command structure' which eventually led to Officers becoming 'apprehensive', no, scared even, to make decisions on the streets when carrying out their lawful duties for fear of being 'disciplined' or even worse, put before a criminal court for trial because the 'reasonable force' used in effecting an arrest was in doubt and many, many more that, in my own opinion, places too much stress on the human body and thus, later in life, leads to health problems and sometimes even death.

I'm not saying that Police Officers should not be accountable because they should but, if they make a decision or carry out an action 'in good faith' and honestly, then they should not be made a 'scapegoat' of, which is where it was heading and that was discouraging Officers whom I saw from making decisions based on the situation they were dealing with and I received many a phone call later in my career from Constables when I was National Crime Recording Standards Sergeant (N.C.R.S. Sgt) concerning many situations they were at or had just been to and asking for my advice as to what action to take or if it had been correct which was to make me an 'enemy' of the bosses and 'command' structure ranks which I will go into further later on in this book because my advice was not always what the 'powers that be' wanted, and I would ALWAYS endorse it on the incident logs to cover the Constables backs from criticism and/or disciplinary action if I felt that they were genuine and proper.

Some 'bosses' (Inspectors, Chief Inspectors, Superintendents) were merely in the Police to progress their career to the next rank above and would 'make examples' of staff or change something that was fine, purely to make a 'name' for themselves and be able to use the 'examples' in their promotion system portfolios which had the effect of demoralising Officers on the streets because they were becoming 'afraid' of taking action.

If you called a Police Officer to your aid, wouldn't you expect them to take control of the situation rather than being worried of doing so because of excessive 'scrutinisation'?

I know I would.

Many good cops died before ever reaching their retiring age of thirty years service or fifty five years of age, whichever came first and now they are expected to Police your streets until they reach the age of sixty which I believe is disgusting because the Police, like other 'services' are not an ordinary vocation and many, many personal sacrifices are made and risks, some life threatening, taken, which the general public rarely get to know about such as compulsory overtime of several hours before they will earn pay (I think it was four hours in a shift week before the time after that would be paid i.e. the first four hours would not be remunerated to the Officer so that could be sixteen hours in a calendar month of working for no pay and I doubt many jobs have to do that do they?)

I witnessed on numerous occasions, Police Officers being injured on duty as a result of assaults, disturbances etc and also, sadly one Officer who nearly died in a Police vehicle accident en route to a 999 call for help.

Many, many times, whilst my family were growing up, we had to rearrange Christmas Day for Boxing Day or even later than that because I, like so many other Officers, had to work those 'special' days.

Yes, we were compensated with double time, but I, like so many other colleagues, would have much preferred to spend the days at home with our families, but we could not, we HAD to work to protect others.

The rate of pay for that sacrifice is not the same now, having been 'eroded' by Government 'cut backs', yet the COMPULSARY REQUIREMENT TO WORK IS.

Back to my role on the Foxtrot Division, I remember one tour of duty when the main road through the centre literally became a 'riot' zone and myself and seven colleagues were trying to fend off a running battle with members of a well known drug gang who were responsible for many armed robberies involving firearms (guns) and were most definitely dangerous criminals.

It felt like 'General Custards last stand' (if you can picture that) and was all brought about by these 'crims' (criminals) being out on a 'social night', probably celebrating another successful robbery and being refused access to a pub, the name of which fails me at this time, but anyway, they decided they were being served and helped themselves, completely 'trashing' the pub in the process!

So, the call for Police was made as they left and went further along the road to another pub which had been pre warned and closed both its solid wood doors, but they (the crims), opened them by force leaving one hanging from its hinges and the other on the floor.

That night we were only eight, which consisted of one Sgt and seven Constables and so, knowing who they were and, more importantly, what they were capable of, we had to make a 'plan of action' to deal with them safely.

It was decided that we would all go to the public house and assess the situation, whilst at the same time, request 'back up' from other sub divisions (a division is the main area Policed which is then divided into sub divisions of which the Foxtrot, at that time, consisted of three, call signs Foxtrot one, two and three).

I didn't hold up much hope of any 'back up' coming after my own personal experience of that, but we had to ensure as much safety as possible and this was before members of 'The Crown' were subjected to those sometimes stupid rules(Health & Safety) which were more 'red tape' restricting our actions on the streets.

The main offender I shall refer to as 'E' and his surname I will refrain from divulging, but he was an extremely dangerous hardened criminal whose respect for another human being was negligible and we agreed it was going to take more than eight of us to bring him down that night, especially if he was 'high' on drugs as well as alcohol, despite seven of us being fellas and that is not meant to sound sexist whatsoever, however one female Constable whom I refer to as Constable Dooley had other ideas.

Again, as with the first pub was also trashed and as we arrived, they were all leaving, till and contents in their possession too.

We had already drawn our 'staffs' and when they saw us, all hell broke loose.

They, and many others, came at us and the call for 'assistance' went out (where you ask for every available police officer from your Division and others nearby, to make their way and this included 'dog handlers with their animals').

It seems to be the case in disorder situations, trouble comes from doorways, alleys, houses etc and before you know it, you are TOTALLY surrounded (hence custards last stand) and you are totally outnumbered.

Constable Dooley decided that she was going to have the 'collar' (arrest) of 'E' and, despite our previously agreeing he would 'come in' (be arrested) when we could safely do that, Constable Dooley made her own decision and grabbed hold of him!

We all knew that he could, and probably would, kill Constable Dooley on her own and so whoever we were on (apprehending), we left to go to the assistance of her and to this day I cannot believe the stupidity of her actions, purely to gain notoriety by effecting the arrest of a dangerous criminal.

Still no 'back up', but we could hear sirens far away and just hoped (I prayed), that those sirens were for us.

I was by no way weak, fourteen weeks at Training College hard training and continuing my weight training and fitness afterwards, I was a force to be reckoned with being fifteen stones of hard muscle and fitness and yet, as we all grabbed 'E' one by one, he threw us off!

I was the last one actually holding him because I had gone for him around his neck in an 'approved' strangle hold (all restraints used by officers must be Home Office approved and at that time, my restraint was however, due to other offenders receiving injuries as a result of this type of restraint, in later years it was withdrawn as approved.

As I became aware of my colleagues being removed and of his ability and strength, I made my own safety decision that, 'E' would be arrested at a later time and I was not going to be put in this serious risk of harm because of a colleagues 'glory hunting' actions and so I reluctantly let go of him and as I did so, with as much force as I could muster, pushed him hard away from me so that I had space between us both.

When our 'back up' eventually arrived, Officers were injured, one having broken ribs, another a broken nose and so we had suffered because of Constable Dooley and her actions that night!

I understand that she was 'spoken to' by the Sgt who took no shit whatsoever when it came to our safety especially when she had gone against a 'mutual decision' made.

One dog handler, Constable Braighton ended up with a very serious complaint as a result of that incident and this was also a potential 'criminal investigation' into his actions with his Police dog because, when he let his dog loose, it too was attacked and so he did what was right and proper in the circumstances and used his dog chain to force his animal from the grips of one angry offender.

That males head was split open like an apple being sliced and, when questioned by internal investigations Constable Braighton said, as I understand, "My dogs life was under threat and I am damned if I am going to let my partner be slaughtered by some little shit!" (Perhaps that offender wasn't so little because it is very rare to be able to overpower and almost kill a Police German shepherd!)

Constable Braighton faced an inquiry for his actions that night but, I am glad to say, he was not charged with any criminal offences nor did he face any further disciplinary matters for 'improper actions' and the matter was closed, which, in my opinion, was the correct result recording it as 'reasonable force in the circumstances'.

I can't even imagine what he would have faced now because of all the 'blame culture' within the Police that there is now but I doubt if he would still be an Officer.

One by one, in the weeks that followed, the offenders responsible for that nights disorder who escaped arrest at the time were rounded up and charged with 'Riot', 'Affray' and Public Disorder offences and C.I.D. (Criminal Investigation Department) carried the crimes (wrote them up and progressed them) and completed the appropriate prosecution files which we were all glad of because it would be one hell of a large file to put together and would have taken many hours to compile taking witness statements etc.

In the eighties and early nineties, C.I.D. would have the resources and time to be able to do such things, unlike now when resources are limited.

Many years later, one of the offenders was sent to prison for their involvement in the murder of a security guard on the steps of a town hall using a firearm after a robbery went wrong, so we were lucky in a way on that night.

The report of the Robbery, murder and subsequent identity of the offender was reported on by the media after conviction, but I am sure that, by reading this, you could make an 'educated guess'.

Throughout my years of service, I have seen many an Investigation commence from the scene of a crime to an offender appearing at court and, I am very pleased to say, the way things are now done has changed for the better by liaison with the C.P.S. (Crown Prosecution Service) BEFORE any charges are laid and rules for investigating crimes where a Constable must complete a complex enquiry and record and retain anything (no matter how small) that could be seen to be evidential in any way.

In the past, many items of 'evidence' had the potential to be disregarded and NEVER USED in court (The recent Hillsborough Enquiry is proof of such 'wrongdoings' and I believe that ALL individuals who are shown to have 'lost' items or 'changed' statements or 'disregarded' potential evidence should, in the public interest, be held accountable for their actions or lack of them and prosecuted accordingly should it be proven to have been purposely done).

My heart goes out to all the families and friends of all the victims of Hillsborough who have been in a living nightmare ever since until corrected earlier in 2012 for all they have ever wanted is Truth and Justice which is something extremely close to my heart which I have always believed in and was a major influence in my ill health retirement as previously referred to.

One investigation which I recall with great sadness was an allegation of Rape made at an enquiry desk on the Foxtrot Three sub Division.

I witnessed the female victim of this horrendous crime report the matter at the enquiry counter (which, in itself takes a great deal of courage), only to be taken by Constable Dooley into the Sergeants office at the far end of the corridor and then the door was closed behind them.

Silence ensued for the next ten minutes or so, presumably whilst the victim explained to the officer what had happened and then, after this, the silence was broken by Constable Dooley shouting at the victim about lying and I remember hearing "If you are lying, you will be dealt with and sent to prison! Do you want to think about what you're saying again because I (Constable Dooley) think you are lying! "

This was the 'old style' of policing and investigation work of the time but to me, it was TOTALLY WRONG and I, from my early career days, would not be a part of such policing and would carry out my duties correctly, protecting Truth and Justice whilst fighting Corruption and Lies!

Quite correctly, in my opinion, I objected about this way of treating a victim of crime to my Sgt (the alcoholic) who was very quick to put me down with "None of your business son, keep out or else face my wrath" and in those 'bad times', the Sgt was in charge of you and what was done, was done!

As a young probationer you could not change that view because no one of any rank would listen to you but they could very easily crush you and 'dispense of your services'.

The first two years a new Constable went through were called 'probationary' for that exact reason, you were on probation and you could be 'dismissed' with little or no reason whatsoever and your chances of appealing this were poor to say the very least!

It was a time where you had to prove yourself to your bosses and that I would do, BUT, in the right way!

CHAPTER FIVE – FOXTROT THREE.

The second part of my probation was spent at the other police station on the Foxtrot three sub Division and the difference in people I dealt with, both criminals and law abiding citizens was amazing in comparison and it was only three and a half miles away.

There was a little more respect for you as a Police Officer, but don't get me wrong, there were still crimes being committed by offenders who didn't give a damn about victims and the effects of their actions upon them and it was my job to give a damn and do my best to support these decent people by arresting the offenders and placing them into the criminal justice system.

Once I had done that, my role was done, after all, a Police Officer IS NOT and MUST NEVER BE, Judge and Jury because that is what a court system and jurors are there for and so I would merely do my utmost to collate all potential evidence, compile it into a structured case and present it to the prosecutors and thus, the courts.

If, after a trial, the Magistrates or Jury (at Crown Court) found a suspect whom I had put before them, not guilty, then that was the end of the matter because I had done everything honestly and correctly and had not and most certainly would not 'bend the rules' or 'stitch someone up', which, sadly I have to say, did occur where certain Constables were concerned and I remember, quite shockingly, two Police Officers being arrested whilst on duty and placed into the cells at the Police station, for doing exactly that.

The matter, again, had been fully reported in the media and the circumstances were that a suspect had been found 'not guilty' at court for an offence of theft from a motor vehicle where he had allegedly stolen a full set of car wheels during one night and the Officers decided that they would take the law into their own hands and re- steal the wheels back from the alleged offender after the courts had returned them to him.

This they did, in a signed Police vehicle, whilst on night shift on the Foxtrot one sub division and a member of public, quite rightly, thought that the sight of two uniformed cops removing wheels from a motor vehicle during the night was not quite right and reported it.

The matter was dealt with extremely well and the wheels were returned to the acquitted man whilst the Officers were arrested on duty by supervising officers. One officer was charged with the theft and I believe, convicted at court whilst the other whom, at the time of the offence, was still 'in company' (with a tutor Constable to show them how to Police) and apparently gave an account similar to he did not know that this was wrong because his 'tutor' had given him a 'legitimate' reason for their actions that night.

Police Officers must be honest law abiding citizens not 'thugs' or 'criminals' in a uniform and are there to uphold the law and NOT to make or break it.

I had a 'new' patch to patrol, still on foot, but somewhat larger in size and I had a new set of colleagues to work with.

The 'relief' (group) at my new station were much younger in service, the most senior having only six years in 'the job' and so that was an 'eye opener' for me because experience only comes with service done, however it was said and I can honestly agree with it that 'If you can survive your probation in an inner city area, then you can complete the whole of your career anywhere because of the experience and variety of incidents you would deal with in those first two years'.

I was concerned that, should I need guidance, then it may not be available because all the relief was inexperienced really, with me being the least experienced.

On one occasion, myself and a female colleague were patrolling on nights when we checked out the rear of a public house because we saw lights in the doorway and figures stood nearby. When we alighted the vehicle, we were met by two males, one of whom was the landlord, who were trying to take us away from the doorway for a reason soon to be divulged.

We made sure that we went to the door and saw another male lying on the floor and appeared to be 'snoring'.

He was found to be the brother of one of the males and we were told that he had had too much to drink and was just 'sleeping it off' whilst the landlord and the other male chatted and that they were going to get him in a taxi but we had driven up.

The way things worked back in the Eighties was that whoever came across an incident or was allocated it over the radio would be the one to deal with it and at that time, I was in my second year of probation and my colleague had four and a half years service in and so was the 'senior' of the two of us and so she took control.

After satisfying herself that the males accounts were viable, she said goodbye and we drove away and to this day I regret that action because we later were called back to the premises by our 'comms' (communication radio control room) only to find C.I.D. present and the same 'sleeping' snoring male dead.

According to the events that transpired, the male was, in fact, drunk but he then fell over and banged his head on the concrete step of the rear door of the public house and when we drove up in the Police vehicle, the landlord and the brother of the deceased were deciding what to do and 'panicked' when we attended, making up their story as they told my colleague.

The 'snoring' was in fact, a sign of a severe head trauma, which I did not know and only wish, at that time, I had known because perhaps things may have turned out differently.

I did, however, utilise that knowledge many years later whilst off duty when an elderly lady was knocked over and thrown some twenty feet into a park in the region where I lived and I immediately recognised her 'snoring' as a sign of head trauma and did everything possible, with the help of a new trainee nurse and a fireman, to try and save her life but unfortunately, our efforts were in vain and she sadly passed away, which deeply upset me and still does to this date, may she rest in peace.

Night shifts really were when you could do what Policing was all about and catch offenders hopefully in the act of committing crimes, however there were times when I became dismayed with certain colleagues who 'went too far'.

One occasion was when my colleague, Constable Drayton and I were on patrol on the Foxtrot three sub Division one foggy night and came across a stolen motor vehicle being driven by two offenders?

Initially we were some distance away and followed the car for some half a mile or so where we could only see the tail lights but as we got closer and checked the Vehicle Registration Plates (V.R.N.) on the Police National Computer (P.N.C.), we confirmed that this car had been reported stolen by its owner and so we attempted to stop it utilising the 'Police Stop' sign on the front of our vehicle and flashing our headlamps at the two occupants.

Obviously, as expected, the vehicle increased speed and we were 'in pursuit'.

At no point could we see who the occupants were and our other 'mobile' colleagues were some distance away and so all we could do was to try and stay with the stolen car until others joined us, but this was not to happen and we continued, at speed, behind it.

The stolen car became faster and faster and at one point we lost sight of it, only to turn a corner and find that it had crashed into some trees and bushes and the offenders had alighted and 'gone to ground' (hidden themselves away to avoid capture).

The road where they had crashed was very straight and lined with trees and shrubbery and so they must have lost control of it as they went around the corner where we had lost our visual on them and so we requested a 'dog handler' to attend to 'track' (this is where the Police dog smells the vehicle seats and then hunts down the offenders using its extremely good sense of smell), however no dog patrol was available and so, as far as we were concerned, the hunt was over even before it had started.

That would have been the case until we saw two dark figures several hundred yards away from us come out of the trees and shrubbery and run across the road away from us.

Obviously, we gave chase on foot and arrested two males on suspicion of stealing the motor vehicle, but, all we had at that time was what was known as 'circumstantial evidence' which was sufficient to justify their arrest, but not sufficient to convict them at court and that was where we were heading.

The decision was made by the 'custody Sgt' (the officer responsible for the welfare of any persons arrested and brought into custody to be interviewed) at that time to charge the suspects with the theft and put them before the courts to decide if they were guilty or not.

The two suspects had denied the offence stating they had been out 'lamping' (where they hunt rabbits and foxes using torches and sometimes dogs), but they could not satisfactorily account for where their equipment was and, despite them both being local to the area, stated that they did not know where they had left their equipment so as you can probably see, there was something not quite right and so the decision to 'let the courts decide' seemed the appropriate action to take.

So the date of trial came because, as expected, both suspects entered pleas of 'not guilty' and so Constable Drayton and I went to Magistrates Courts to give our evidence.

I always believed that it was much better to 'learn my evidence off by heart' before entering the court so that I did not have to refer to my pocket note book (P.N.B.) and so I would read it whilst waiting outside the court room and then put it away.

If required, I could always refer to it in the courtroom and it was always available to the magistrates, prosecution, defence or suspects to look at should they wish because my notes were always written up 'as soon as practicable' and I always aimed to do this at the very latest, within an hour of the incident or arrest whilst it was still very fresh in my mind.

In my opinion, the 'evidence' was insufficient to convict the suspects and I had resigned myself to them both being 'acquitted' and walking away and that did not concern me because, if there was insufficient evidence to convict, then so be it, they would commit further offences, they were known to the Police and the next time, we would hopefully have evidence to complete the process.

I was totally shocked when Constable Drayton then suggested to me that "we could say they were in the car and that we saw them run from it after crashing and running into the shrubbery and trees".

I immediately asked him to 'run that by me again', thinking I had misheard this Constable who, up until that point, had always seemed to me to be a genuine and honest copper, but he said the same to me again.

My response was "I will go into that courtroom and swear upon oath (on the Holy Bible if, as I was, baptised as Church of England) to tell 'the truth, the whole truth and nothing but the truth' and that was that they were NOT seen running away from the stolen car and that we had NOT seen who the occupants were and that we HAD lost sight of the vehicle and when we found it again it had crashed and was EMPTY".

Constable Drayton was disappointed and began telling me that we were all 'on the same side' and that our purpose was to 'put these car thieves behind bars' and also that this 'would not go well with other cops' if I didn't go with it.

Obviously, I was annoyed with him and so I said "I will say this only once because if I have to say it again, it will be after I have punched you to the floor. I am an honest cop and pride myself with that fact and if you wish to lie about this, on oath, then I will let you know now, I will say exactly how it occurred and, if asked, will say that you are lying and will come to see you in prison only once to tell you what a stupid pillock you are!"

Constable Drayton thought about this for a while and then walked away from me in disgust. He was then called in to give his evidence and I followed some twenty minutes later, not knowing whether he had lied or told the truth as it had occurred, but, if he had lied on oath, I would soon find out.

Fortunately for Constable Drayton, he told the truth as did I and the outcome was the two suspects were found 'not guilty' and acquitted.

This was right and proper, but made me an 'enemy within' and several colleagues refused to speak to me for some time, including Constable Drayton.

I have always had certain 'beliefs' within me which I would ALWAYS strive to maintain and these are:-

- I believe that ALL humans are equal and should be treated as such without favour or malice.
- Nobody should be discriminated against because of their gender or race.
- Cruelty against children should NEVER be tolerated, no excuses.
- I will never tolerate violence against females.
- Honesty is ALWAYS the best policy.

On an afternoon shift I was called to an address where the lives of one family would never to be the same again and this touched my heart in a way I would never forget.

The call was to a serious sexual assault on a female and when we arrived, a lady who was a mother of two and a wife, had been raped and sodomised whilst walking home after an evening out with friends.

This lady had been no more than half a mile away from her home when she was attacked from behind and dragged screaming down a back alley and yet nobody heard her cries, something that made me doubt 'human spirit' because it was a populated area with houses and pubs on the road where she had been.

To make matters even worse, I didn't think that they could be at that time but they were, this lady had been menstruating and had screamed this at the attacker who did not give a damn and this really sickened me to the bone because it was the first sexual offence I had personally dealt with and all I could think of was that I had a wife and how would this affect me if she were the victim of such a sickening attack?

My own human emotions had to be put aside, which I have to say was extremely hard, and I had to remain professional and so I called for C.I.D. to attend together with a female Officer because it was always best practise to utilise an Officer of the same sex to speak to the victim of this type of crime (so long as they weren't treated like the earlier victim with Constable Dooley but I am glad to say, times were changing and victims were receiving a little 'improved' treatment).

Matters took time and resources because we had to identify the scene of the attack to preserve it for forensic examination, make enquiries at the houses around the scene and, most importantly, get an accurate description of the offender and circulate this on our P.R. (personal radio) for other patrols to look out for with the hope of taking this male off the streets as soon as possible and prevent any further attacks from happening.

At the victims address was her husband who, quite rightly, had emotions that were on a rollercoaster, tears, frustration, anger and the like and who wouldn't be after their most loved had just been violated in the worst possible way and I was stood at the front door when he burst out intent on finding and killing the offender!

I had to act fast and so I stood in his way and a 'heated' conversation occurred between us as I tried, in vain, to placate him.

What happened next, I was most certainly NOT anticipating.

The husband calmed down, started to breathe slower and then, unbeknown to me, clenched his fist and before I could anticipate and react to this, he punched me hard across my chin, knocking my helmet off my head and it felt like my jaw bone had been sent across my face like in a cartoon and then back into place.

Before he could make off to 'kill' the offender if he found him (to be honest, I think at that point, any male would have done because he just needed a pressure release, his emotions were in turmoil and overdrive), I grabbed hold of him by his arms with both my hands, forcibly pinned him against the outside wall of his home and screamed at him that his wife needed him and that I could totally understand his anger but, if he took the law into his own hands, that would not help the lady he loved.

He slowly calmed down and so I let him go, picked up my helmet and said "that was 'on the house', but if you do not heed my advice, I may have to act accordingly and how the hell will that help your wife who is inside and needs you by her side so very much now, so go back inside ok?"

That was the end of the matter as far as I was concerned and the investigative wheels continued and within one hour an arrest was made by an astute colleague on patrol of a male who fitted the offenders description, but unfortunately, it was a case of 'mistaken identity' and he was released after his alibi was confirmed and I retired from duty later.

The following evening, I had a caller to the enquiry counter and it was the husband who wished to apologise for hitting me the previous night and stating he must be dealt with for his actions.

This was where Constable Spence was influenced by Mitchell Spence and I told him "I'm sorry sir, I do not recall you hitting me", to which the man asked if I was the Officer who had attended his address the night before which obviously I confirmed.

He then seemed confused and reaffirmed his account to which I again said "I'm sorry sir, I do recall attending your address and speaking to you but I DO NOT recall you hitting me whatsoever!

I recall our having a conversation about how you could help and support your wife after a serious assault had happened and then you went inside and I left".

The penny then dropped for this man that I was not going to prosecute him for an act which he carried out whilst extremely emotionally traumatised and that, if he continued to insist he had hit me, I would still disagree and so the matter would end there and then.

When he understood my 'angle' on this, he thanked me from the bottom of his heart and I winked at him and said "now you need to go back home to your wife whom it is obvious you love and care about because she needs all your support now and that of your family".

The law would be totally wrong if I was compelled to arrest this man for the assault he committed against me whilst under extreme distress and that was the only time I had denied something that had occurred and I believe I can be forgiven for my act of humanity on that occasion, don't you?

Whilst stationed on the Foxtrot Division, I was trained for 'operational support' which is where the police force you belonged to could be called upon for 'mutual aid' whereby you could be sent to other forces should they need more officers to cope with extra demands such as disorder or dignitaries visiting etc and on one occasion we were called to Tewksbury which is policed by Gloucestershire Constabulary because there had been an incident where the Police had, as I recall, fatally wounded a member of the ethnic minorities and they had had information that, on the day of a demonstration to object to the shooting, a group of protestors were intent on 'storming' the local Police station and burning it to the ground and so, very early one morning we were sent in a P.S.U. (Police Support Unit) consisting of one Inspector, three Sergeants and eighteen Constables of which I was one.

The orders we were given were that the protestors were going to do everything possible to provoke Officers there into a disorder situation so that they (the protestors) could claim Police harassment and hopefully make the front pages of the newspapers illustrating what the Police were all about which in their minds was violence against ethnic minorities and so we were told that, at no cost, were we to react to provocation, no matter how intense it was and also that, at all costs, we were to prevent anyone from breaking through our lines to attack the local Police station.

We all formed 'open' cordons (human barriers where we would stand in normal uniform with spaces between each Officer) and should the need occur, we would then reinforce these with a second open cordon behind but between so that the spaces were filled but in a staggered way by more Officers.

Many Police forces sent a P.S.U that day because this was a severe threat to 'authority' and could not be allowed to occur and in some areas, it did become somewhat agitated, but fortunately not in my immediate locality and we all know that disorder doesn't take much to spark when you look back through 2010 to 2012, but this was in the late Eighties and fortunately, effectively Policing the streets was still possible.

I remember very well, a well built black man walking along our lines staring directly into our faces attempting to provoke action by calling us 'scum, pigs, filth, murderers, bastards' and much more, but we had our orders....no reaction to anything whatsoever and believe me, when you are directly threatened verbally or physically, it is extremely hard to be placid, but that is what we were there to do and, so long as my orders were not illegal or would subject me to disciplinary action, then I would and did, obey them which is what is expected of anyone who serves the public and represents 'The Crown'.

My turn came for his abuse and, whether it was because I was tall or younger than him, he stopped immediately in front of me and stared.

His body language was aggressive, his eyes were hardened and, to be perfectly honest with you, he scared the shit out of me!

He was so close to my face that I could smell his rancid tobacco breath and could see his scars on his face from previous dealings with a blade or blades and he just spoke firmly, quietly and aggressively, waiting for me to respond.

I was always taught that, if someone tries to 'stare you out' eye to eye, then you must look at their forehead or hairline because then you still look as if you are eye to eye but, in fact, you are not.

It is human nature to avoid eye contact in potential violent situations and a human being has a natural 'comfort zone' of approximately two feet around them and should someone come closer than that, you naturally feel 'threatened or intimidated or just un-comfy (unless, of course, you know them or are about to hug or kiss them).

The male sniggered at me, looked me up and down and then said "Die you murderous bastard!"

You can probably understand how I was feeling at that exact moment and it was very obvious, by my helmet badge, that I was an 'outsider' from another Force area and not a local from Gloucestershire Police and perhaps that is why this male chose me to attempt to intimidate.

Time seemed to stop for me because my natural action would be to warn the male off, take a few steps back to allow me a 'safe zone' from which I could react and defend myself and there was no such thing as 'body armour', C.S. Spray or side handled batons then, all I had was my wits and a truncheon or staff.

I was extremely aware that this male could have a weapon and could be wanting to kill a Police Officer to make the protestors 'even' so to speak, but I still held my pacif stand looking ahead at his forehead until, eventually, he moved off to try his luck with another Police 'victim', what relief I felt at that moment!

We were successful with our given objective, the Police station was not 'stormed' and we were 'stood down' after a very long tour of duty, to return back to our own Police area and how glad I was of that too.

Anyone who ever says that they have never been scared at some point in their career as a Police Officer is a complete LIAR because there will always be a point where they face something that 'un-nerves' them or makes them fearful, after all, fear is a human characteristic, we all have a natural in-build instinct of 'fight or flight' as do all animals, mammals and possibly insects that have intelligence and it is in situations like that where your true strength comes out, will you stand and fight or will you run in flight?

There was a great camaraderie in my initial years as a Police Officer but that changed as we entered the mid nineties and early millennium as I have touched upon slightly earlier in this book and will elaborate on further in so I hope that you will stay with me throughout.

Car crime was at its high really in the Nineties, with the inner city Divisions being hit the hardest by criminals intent on stealing the latest 'Phillips' car stereos or alloy wheels which were now being fitted to the 'nicer' motor cars, not forgetting stealing cars merely to 'joy-ride' in them although that terminology did not reflect what really happened because, if a car was stolen and driven by thieves, it was either used to 'bait' Police mobile patrols into chasing them where the consequences could be grave if the stolen car crashed or the patrol saw 'red mist' (which is when you lose your reality because your aim is to catch the offenders no matter what and happens without you consciously realising it on many occasions), which led later in time to new rules concerning Police pursuits (saving lives of Police Officers, criminals and, most importantly, innocent members of the public) or it was used in a 'ram-raid'(where two vehicles are stolen and one is used to drive through a shop frontage usually an electrical store and the other vehicle is filled with stolen property and used for the criminals escape).

The sentencing for such crimes never reflected the damage or property stolen and I honestly believe that this was because the judicial system (courts) felt that a crime against a business was less important than a crime against an individual for which you could argue for and against in debating this.

Businesses, yes, had insurance to pay for the losses, but businesses also had individuals who owned them and so suffered because of the crime or crimes and so, because the sentencing did not fit the crime, (yes, similar to the judicial system of today, however, the present system could owe its origin to yesterdays sentencing couldn't it?), the offences continued to increase in number and frequency.

The main offenders on the Foxtrot three sub-division were no more than six to eight in numbers, but, were responsible for most, if not all, of the related car crimes recorded and, had they been sentenced to prison, then, in my own opinion, the crimes would have fallen or even stopped (at least whilst they were 'inside'- in prison).

Vauxhall Cavalier Sri, Ford Fiesta XR2 or XR2i vehicles as well as Ford Escort XR3 or 3i were the chosen 'favourites' of this 'crew' and they would entice or taunt the Police by driving them in an erratic manner and leaving their 'calling card' which consisted of rubber tyre circles caused by 'wheel-spinning' on the main arterial routes around the sub-division, especially, believe it or not, near the Police station and their homes.

At the time, it was normal practise for a Police Officer to drive a stolen recovered vehicle into the Police station where it would be booked into the 'property system' and the owner would be notified to collect same.

A Ford Escort XR3i was brought into the station and secured in the rear yard but the thieves obviously did not wish to let their claim on the vehicle go that evening because, after the Officer had 'booked it in', he returned outside to where the vehicle had been parked and found that it had been re-stolen!

Can you believe it? We were astounded that the thieves had had the 'balls' to enter the rear of the Police station yard and re-steal the vehicle and it took them no more than five minutes because that is how long the Officer was away completing the necessary paperwork. The embarrassment I expect he felt too when he had to contact the owner to tell them that their pride and joy had been recovered but then stolen from right under the eyes of the Police.

Needless to say, soon after this incident, cameras were placed in the rear yards of most stations to prevent a reoccurrence.

In December, 1991, I received a Chief Constable's Commendation,(the highest in force bravery award), for my actions one night which were described as 'Tenacious, Brave and illustrating Great Courage' and a night that caused me extreme stress and upset for many years and still does occasionally (this would be diagnosed as Post Traumatic Stress Disorder nowadays) because on that night shift, I honestly believed that I was to die in a dark, cold, alley on my own after having been subjected to a ferocious and violent attack for carrying out my duties and attempting to effect an arrest of a male whom I was later informed was an 'enforcer' for a well known Drugs gang.

At this time my wife was pregnant and my other child was only eighteen months or so old and those thoughts were with me throughout my ordeal which, even now, some twenty one years later, causes my eyes to well up with tears because I might have not seen them grow up or shared my life with my wonderful lady had it not been for the professionalism that my colleagues out on the street, especially my Sgt whom I refer to as Sgt Pearce and in the comms (radio room), Constable Knight, for they were there for me when I NEEDED them the most and I cannot ever thank them enough for that.

I was on a routine mobile patrol on the Foxtrot three sub division when I came across a male whom I knew was disqualified by a court from driving and here he was behind the wheel of a Ford Fiesta vehicle so I did what I was there to do, prevent offences, protect the public and arrest criminals and began to follow the car whilst radioing in to my comms where I was and what was happening.

This male whom I will call Joney, continued to drive in front of me and when I illuminated the 'stop' sign on the front of my vehicle and flashed my headlamps indicating for him to stop, he behaved as I expected and increased speed and away he went.

I called in the fact he had failed to stop and continued to pursue him, quite surprisingly, all the way to his council flat where he stopped outside!

This did not ring right with me and so I was a little cautious and remained in my car behind 'K' and indicated for him to get out which, no surprise here, he did not.

Joney slammed his car into reverse and deliberately 'rammed' my Police vehicle and then, as I radioed this in, quite shocked, he then sped off again and we went around a small 'island' in the cul-de-sac where he lived, twice, each time his speed increasing until I was now involved in a full scale pursuit but still on my own because my colleagues were several minutes behind my last location and started to 'guess' which way I may go next.

The comms operator, Constable Knight, was constantly updating patrols via myself as to where I was heading and what was occurring, yet still I was on my own and then, after turning a bend in the road, I came across the fiesta crashed with its nearside wheel bent under at the roadside and Jonesy and another, still inside it!

The next moments seemed like an eternity and yet, I am sure it was only a matter of maybe ten or fifteen minutes before my ordeal finished, but by the end of it, I was totally concussed, confused and extremely disorientated.

Joney alighted from his vehicle in what I can only describe as an utter rage and began to move towards me with a face full of anger and so I started to alight from my Police vehicle but before I could get fully out, although I was now standing up between the car door and the body, he used the full force of his foot to slam the car door into my body and I was now pinned in unable to escape (the force he used actually dented the car door into a 'v' shape).

I was then subjected to an intense bout of punches and, despite my every effort to free myself, could not and so had no option but to be punched hard and fast to my head and upper body!

When I did manage to get my arms free, I still could not get a punch in and couldn't understand why this was but I was later to be informed by my Inspector that Joney had been an amateur boxer and that is why I stood no chance to return anything in self defence.

I did manage to eventually push myself free of the car door and again attempt to defend myself, but was sent to the floor by yet another punch from Joney!

At this point, unbeknown to me, the incident was being witnessed from nearby by a local resident who later, it was their evidence at Crown Court was to be the evidence to secure a conviction because, and I can fully understand this from my previous accounts of how Officers had been, as time went on, 'trust' in a Police Officers' evidence was being questioned which did actually sadden me somewhat because I was, from the very start until the very end of my career, an Honest Cop.

I attempted to make some space between Joney and I and so, on all fours (hands and knees), I scrambled my way along the public road looking over my shoulder as best I could as I did and shouted "Joney, what are you doing you bloody fool!"

I am glad that I did because, by shouting his name, he knew that I knew who he was and, for a couple of seconds, a look of caution seemed to appear on his face and he momentarily ceased his hostilities which was enough time for me to draw my staff (truncheon), get up from my knees and start to run at him with it raised in the air! (Why, you ask, when I have just been quite severely assaulted on duty by a hardened criminal? well, because he was going to go to court for what he had done to me and nothing would prevent me from arresting him for that, despite my being somewhat confused now, THAT was why!)

Joney then turned on his feet and ran and I followed, totally unaware of where the passenger from his car was, until he went down a dark alleyway and I followed.

The last radio message I heard was "where are you, what's your location?" and as I carried on running, I then saw Joney stop ahead of me, turn around, clench his fists and, in a rage scream something like "You're gonna have it now!"

I tried to radio my location which was nowhere near my car now, but, as I did so, I was ferociously attacked and my radio and I lost touch!

My staff raised high in the air above my head, I swung down hard and fast but as I did so, It was grabbed from behind, by the other occupant of the car preventing my connecting with Joney and at that point, as I turned and tried to pull the staff from the other assailant, Joney punched and kicked me several times causing me to feel extreme pain and discomfort and it was at this point that I heard the message on my radio which by now was on the floor out of my reach "Mitchell, what is your location?" and then, after I had not responded "Mitchell, for Gods' sake, where are you?" "Patrols make your way ASAP to the last known location please!"

I felt, at that exact moment, that I was never going to see my family again because, by now, my staff had been grabbed from me and was coming down at me in the hand of Joney straight towards my head!

In sheer desperation, I raised my right arm to deflect any blow to my head which I have no doubt was the Joneys intention and would, I am quite certain, have split my head in two.

My staff connected with full force, across my right hand and the pain I felt was excruciating, but I would not give in, Joney was not going to get away with it and again, from behind, I felt myself being pulled, the second assailant yet again.

I fought to the best of my capabilities in my defence against both these offenders and ended up on the cold, damp floor but still I would not be beaten and so I grabbed hold of both legs of Joney and tried to bring him down to no avail and my strength by now was ebbing and the thought of being beaten to death was right at the forefront of my mind, this was not how I wanted to die, not here on a cold damp floor in the darkness, after all, many years ago I had been given a 'second chance' and this should not be happening to me this way.

My family, safe in bed at home, was all I could see in my mind and that, I feel, hurt me more than the physical injuries I had received from these offenders and to this day, at that point, I can only believe that it was the injustice prevailing that gave me the extra strength to keep hold, not knowing if I had any 'assistance' coming or, in fact, if they actually knew where I was!

Joney was trying his very best to release my grip and eventually he went down, where I was, on the floor, so I suppose that 'evened' things up a little, but I was too tired to fight now and felt sure that, very soon, my grip would fail and I would then die because he wouldn't leave me to identify him would he?

Moments after this I heard several feet 'pounding' down the alley way towards me and these were from both sides, it was my colleagues under instruction from Sgt Pearce, who had made an educated guess as to my location and had 'front and backed' the alley way (blocking both entry and exit routes)and were now almost with me!

Sgt Pearce shouted at me "let him go now Mitchell, we've got him, you can move away", which, with extreme relief, I did by rolling away and staggering to my feet and my colleagues took over with Sgt Pearce ordering them all "Nobody hits him, he's going down (to prison) for what he has done to Mitchell!".

Joney was then handcuffed, as was the other assailant who turned out to be his drug addict girlfriend of all people (she had the strength of an Ox that night and I could not believe it was her) and I was then helped back to my car which I drove back to the Police station.

Driving a vehicle after such an assault would not happen now and probably shouldn't have happened back then because I was a danger to myself and others with concussion and dizziness, I could have passed out at any time, but that was the way it was, the car door couldn't even close because it had been so badly dented and so I drove back very slowly.

Ironically, there used to be a night club on the main road called 'Hardy's' and, as I drove past it, a group were fighting and then, when they saw me, began to scream abuse and make threats, so I SLOWED DOWN TO STOP!

I wasn't thinking straight and as soon as I had almost stopped, I drove off again because, well I am sure that I could be forgiven, I had just had the shit kicked out of me.

When I was driven to hospital, I couldn't speak properly or think straight and my Inspector had to give my details to the Hospital staff who, after examining me, stated I was suffering from symptoms of having been 'punch drunk' like Boxers do after a big fight and so that explained things a little (not that I could rationalise them at that time).

My right hand was badly bruised and swollen but, fortunately, not broken, however it was bandaged and put into a sling and that was to be the end of my Policing for the next six weeks, but at least I could enjoy my family, the family I thought I would never see again!

I was driven home later in the morning and a colleague drove my personal car. My wife saw my car being driven home without me in it and then a Police vehicle with another driver in and so you can just imagine the thoughts going through her mind when she had expected me home at 7 in the morning, I had not called, and here at 9 in the morning, was my car being driven by someone other than me with a Police car following.

That is every spouse's nightmare because their loved one, well, where are they?

When I came around the corner with my hand bandaged and in a sling, I could see that she was shocked, but, more importantly, relieved that I was alive and home.

I certainly did not wish to experience that again, but this was an inner city Division and so, no doubt, risk would rear its ugly head again at some point.

When I did return back to work, I had a first-hand 'good cop, bad cop' experience with a male whom I shall refer to as 'night walker' and a colleague of mine who decided several years later, that he had 'had enough' of the Police, despite having fifteen years service, and so he resigned and became a bus driver in the Lake District I am led to believe.

I have to say that his decision to resign was a good one because, in my opinion, he was becoming somewhat 'unpredictable' and I certainly do not think he would have stayed 'sane' as the Police changed.

Anyway, we had been plagued for weeks by 'malicious' 999 calls about fires, accidents and public disorder on the Foxtrot three sub division all made from public telephone boxes and, because there was no CCTV cameras on town and city centres like there is now, if we weren't quick enough to respond, the offender 'got away with it'.

Every time these calls had been made, we saw the 'night walker' not very far away from the 'scenes' and every time we spoke to him, he gave us false descriptions of the alleged offenders whom he had seen 'running away', coincidentally, just before we arrived.

There was nothing we could do about this because, unless we caught him 'in the act' (committing the offence on the phone), then he was in the clear and he knew it.

The 'night walker' was a lonely man who suffered from insomnia (unable to sleep) and often, when on nights, we and other colleagues, would stop for a chat, falsely believing he was helping us prevent or detect crime and thank him for his information as well which I suppose, made him feel good about himself.

One night, he went too far and we caught him whilst en route (on our way) to another, unconnected call and saw him leaving a call box so we radioed in to allocate our 'job' to another patrol and drove past him and around the corner, hoping that another false 999 call would come through and, most importantly, from the call box where he had just vacated, and it did!

We couldn't believe our luck and immediately approached him and arrested him under the provisions of the 'general arrest conditions', section 25 P.A.C.E. (Police and Criminal Evidence Act, 1984) because his arrest was necessary due to our being unable to ascertain a satisfactory name and address to serve a summons upon him and so he was brought into the Police station to be questioned.

This power has now been 'revoked', BUT, the IDENTICAL powers 'introduced' under section 110 (5) of the Serious Organised Crime and Police Act 2005 (SOCAPA), which I refer to later in this book when I was arrested for malicious allegations made by an Officer who, in my opinion, was a corrupt Police officer.

My colleague was already 'in his face' before he had even been 'booked in' (documented by the custody Sgt), and was firmly indicating to him what he would do to him if he did not tell the truth which I thought was somewhat 'oppressive' and out of order at that time and made my 'objections' known to him.

When it came to interviewing the 'night walker', this was now done on paper with one Officer asking questions and another writing both questions and answers down AT THE TIME, which was so much different to the Officer I referred to earlier in this book writing his notes up on the day of the court trial and this was something that had been brought in under P.A.C.E. and the 'codes of practise' for questioning persons in detention under arrest. The suspect would then be allowed to read and sign the interview notes as accurate if they agreed and if they did not, they were allowed to 'comment' upon the aspects they may feel were incorrect which was much safer and proper for both the suspect AND the Police.

I was to take the notes because I was the 'junior' Officer (less service) but at least I would be able to ensure that this interview was conducted correctly and within the law.

As we brought the suspect from his cell to an interview room, my colleague gave him the 'third degree' again about lying and so I intervened and spoke over him to inform 'night walker' that it was best to tell the truth because we would ascertain all the facts of the incident, no matter how long it took and to be quite honest, the way in which my colleague spoke to the suspect concerned me.

Before we interviewed, my colleague left the room for a few moments and I took the opportunity to inform the suspect that I was concerned by my colleagues demeanour and that he (the suspect) had nothing to fear because I would NOT allow anything to happen to him whilst in custody but that I wanted to know the truth and, if he had committed the offence and any other offences similar, why.

I believe that it was because I had treated him in a right and proper way, civil and within the boundaries of the law, that he decided, eventually, to talk to us and this was amazing because, not only had he committed the offence for which we had arrested him for, but he admitted, factually with dates and times, ALL the other calls that had been made to the emergency services.

We charged him with four offences and had the rest (in excess of ten) taken into consideration (T.I.C.) when he appeared before court and, unlike when C.I.D. would look at offences being put for T.I.C. ours were correct and true whereby, in my opinion, some of their matters and 'detections' could be seen as 'dubious'(explained further in chapter six).

The 'night walker' pleaded guilty to all matters at court and was fined heavily for his trouble, but the good thing that came from this was that it 'turned him around' and he became genuine eyes and ears certainly for me and possibly for some of my other colleagues when working night shift and still made call box calls, the difference being these were genuine and he would wait for us to attend and tell us first-hand what he had seen.

He realised that what he had done was wrong and told me in his own words that he 'wanted to make it right again'.

I certainly had quite a good professional relationship with that man for the rest of my time on the Foxtrot three sub Division!

CHAPTER SIX – PLAIN CLOTHES POLICING.

After serving in uniform for several years, I felt that a change would be as good as a rest and so I applied successfully to join the 'street thefts' department which was where you could deal solely with crime on the streets and hopefully, because of the civilian clothing, be around a crime or crimes when they were committed and thus apprehend the offenders.

I realised, very early on, that ordinary radios were of no use because they 'stood out like a sore thumb' and so I managed to acquire four sets of 'covert' (hidden) radio harnesses and equipment where your transmit button was in your sleeve and your microphone was on your collar or shirt and that, in itself, would allow my colleagues and I to get 'up front and personal' with criminals, yet have the comms readily available to help us if needed.

There was also a tiny 'earpiece' also that fitted snugly in to your ear canal so it could not be seen

I was teamed up with three other Constables and their daily routine seemed simply to be, into work, newspaper reading, drive around or walk for a little while, lunch, maybe into a pub for a drink or two (totally taboo for officers on duty unless express permission given by high ranks so that the officers 'fitted in', which was not the case with these Constables!), then to a sweet shop for some 'goodies' and then back to the station to finish.

This was NOT what I wanted to do, but I was the same rank as they and no-one would give a damn if I made it known, so I started to take out 'warrants' for the arrest of offenders or would just go for a walk on my own and end up arresting a thief or a burglar. This would put the 'spotlight' onto the others who did little and they would then have to do one of two things, get involved or try to stop me from 'rocking the boat' as it was referred and I was having none of the latter.

Eventually, the message got out loud and clear and all four of us would contribute to effective policing and detect some good car crimes and burglaries, much to the frustration of some 'Detective Officers' in C.I.D. because we were now 'treading on their toes' a little bit as they said, but we didn't give a damn and were enjoying being out and about but doing what was supposed to be done, detect offences and prosecute offenders.

One of the things being on 'street thefts' did do for me was to allow me to gain an insight into some of the wrongdoings where 'detections' were concerned when offenders, once charged (placed into the judicial system) with a criminal offence, were 'pressed' by detectives in C.I.D. for admissions to other offences which could then be 'taken into consideration' (T.I.C) by the courts.

Under normal circumstances, this is a legitimate way to detect other crimes committed by an offender when charging them would add no more to their sentence at court but it was subject to abuse by many who had their 'targets' well before the official 'performance targets' of the millennium and present times were ever introduced.

You see, the D.C.I. or D.I. (Detective Chief Inspector or Detective Inspector) would want their staff to regularly supply them with crimes that had been 'detected' by way of T.I.C. and they would then 'hold these back' from monthly submissions unless they were 'under target' and then they would 'slip several through' for detections and hope that they succeeded without being caught.

There was nothing illegal by what they were doing but it was immoral and, should these 'detections' have been obtained by force, fear or fraud, then they were totally liable for all subsequent 'fall- out' from their directions given and I certainly know, from general chatter in the office between Detectives that they all had their 'favourite' criminals who would admit many a crime for them for the price of a 'packet of fags' or a 'good word' with the magistrates and that, when these criminals were arrested by uniform, the 'detective' would go rummaging through all his or her undetected crimes and sort a few for them to admit.

Now that WAS, in my mind, CORRUPT, yet seemed to have the full backing of the D.C.I and D.I. because it kept them 'comfy' with H.Q. (Headquarters Divisional and Force level).

That was all to change one morning with a 'statement' from the then D.C.I. Peterson (as I will refer to him), who was a 'gentleman' but allowed these 'practises to occur.

D.C.I. Peterson spoke to all staff after one of the 'morning read-ups' (where the crimes of the last 24 hours are covered and any progresses made on others) when he said to the effect of "Scrutiny has occurred now at Force level on the way we have crimes detected by way of T.I.C. and so what I am saying really is be careful with when and what you now submit to me because I will be accepting that they are correct as stated and, should things go pear shaped, it is you, the individual who submitted it, that will be accountable, not I".

In his next breath, as he was leaving the office, he said something to the effect of "But I will still expect your regular submissions in similar quantities to normal each month".

What he was saying without actually saying it was, I believe, keep on fiddling the figures as normal, but if caught, you're on your own.

This caused great debates around the office of Detectives and totally amazed me, but nothing changed and they continued this 'mal-practise' which I thought was appalling and I made several comments about this being 'as good as bent' and should not be allowed but that simply 'alienated' me from several Detectives to my disadvantage later in my career when I had an attachment to C.I.D. for six long, hard, lonely months.

Whilst on street thefts, we underwent observations on known criminals, arrested several for Burglaries, Deceptions, Thefts and even 'abstracting electricity' where they had 'bypassed' their electricity meters and gained many a 'conviction' at court by doing things the right and proper way and had many a foot chase with offenders whom were wanted and I really enjoyed the 'freedom' it gave us to go where we wanted and when, but I would never allow myself to become entwined in anything 'dubious' and colleagues knew exactly how I felt about that.

One afternoon I was working with a colleague, Constable Grady, and we were in an Austin Montego plain car looking for offenders, when we saw a known Burglar and car thief drive past us in a B.M.W!

We both knew that he did not have the assets to buy that type of vehicle and he had been disqualified from driving until recently and so we followed him.

I shall refer to this male as Sharpie and he soon came to realise we were on his case and sped up with a view to losing us through the back streets.

Constable Grady was driving and I gave commentary over the radio hoping to get a 'uniform' to join us and stop Sharpie but this was not to occur and Constable Grady and I ended up 'cornering' him in a cul-de-sac where he was trying to turn the BMW around to make off again.

I alighted from our vehicle and ran toward 'M' who by now had turned around and was starting to drive in my direction!

Fearing he was driving at me, I drew my staff into the air and, as the car came towards me, 'slammed' it with as much force as I could muster, into the BMW windscreen causing it to crack and shatter but not fully break.

This was enough to shock Sharpie momentarily and as I then hit the drivers' window with my staff, that completely smashed and I threw myself into the 'cockpit' of the BMW (the driver area) and began struggling with Sharpie in order to effect his arrest.

Constable Grady was still in the unmarked Police vehicle and he saw events unfolding that I was completely 'blind' to because I had my hands full fighting with Sharpie and I was so very grateful that Constable Grady was so astute in his observations and subsequent actions at that time.

As soon as I was into the cockpit, Sharpie pushed his foot flat to the floor and began to accelerate the vehicle whilst struggling with me and I was trying to hit him and take the keys from the ignition thus, totally oblivious to anything else.

As the BMW increased speed, the vehicle was also travelling in the direction of a concrete lamp post and I was half in and half out of the vehicle, my waist and lower body being in direct line to smash into the lamp post and, to this day, I do strongly believe that I would have either been severely paralysed from the waist down or possibly dead from injuries that would most certainly had occurred if Constable Grady had not acted in the way he did.

Constable Grady was facing the BMW as it increased speed and possibly could have tried to reverse away or move, but he did not, he sat and 'braced himself' for an impact that he knew was coming and that could also possibly injure him too because he knew that if he did not, then I could suffer badly and we were, after all, carrying out our duties with the utmost professionalism as expected.

Whilst fighting with Sharpie the inevitable 'impact' occurred and both the Police vehicle and the BMW ended up bonnets smashed and, for a few seconds, pointing slightly skyward with their front wheels off the road surface before banging back down on the floor.

I had managed to turn the BMW keys and cut the engine before impact and the force of this threw me sideways slightly but I kept hold of Sharpie until my colleague, Constable Grady, had recovered his senses and come to my aid.

Obviously we had now had what was known as a P.V.A (police vehicle accident) and so a Sgt was requested to attend the scene as well as a van to take our 'prisoner' away because the Sgt would have to report the matter.

I felt sick and dizzy because I knew, whilst struggling with Sharpie in the moving vehicle, that what was happening was extremely dangerous but I was 'beyond the point of no return' and had I let go, then I could have quite easily fallen beneath the wheels of the BMW as it accelerated.

My emotions were high after seeing how close I had come to impacting with the concrete lamp post- only a matter of three feet away, my breathing quickening and, before I knew it, I was wavering to the point of passing out and so I was helped to the side of the road to sit down and an Ambulance was called for.

I now know this condition to be called 'hyper-ventilation' caused by 'shock' and it is a 'vicious circle' because the more you breathe rapidly, the more oxygen gets into your body and the more confused you feel so your breathing and heart rate continue to increase and then, because of too much oxygen, your outer extremities like hands, feet, legs and arms then experience 'pins and needles'.

This is then followed by confusion, dizziness and finally, if not controlled, collapse!

It is extremely scary when you have experienced this for the first time, yet the 'cure' is simple, a   paper bag covering both your mouth and nose as you breathe in and out.

The bag has to be paper and not plastic, something to do with ratio of gasses I think, not sure, but it works.

This allows more carbon dioxide to remain in your system until the 'balance' is restored to your body and organs, as simple as that, yet, if not treated, it can become very dangerous indeed.

So, after being checked over and treated by the ambulance staff who were excellent, I was allowed to return to my duties and look again and again at how much of a 'close-call' that had been.

Later that day, we interviewed Sharpie about his vehicle and actions and it transpired that the vehicle was indeed legitimately owned by him, but, he had no driving licence, insurance or M.O.T. for the BMW and so he was charged with numerous offences including failing to stop for a Police Officer and reckless driving (now the latter is covered by a change in legislation to dangerous driving) and his account for his actions was that 'he panicked'.

Despite my 'run-ins' with danger, this was the vocation that I (or it) had chosen and I was proud to carry the badge which represented, in my mind, 'Truth and Justice' and I was certainly seeing quite a bit of 'action' whilst carrying out my duties on the Foxtrot Division.

Sooner or later though, you have a 'reality check' and in my mind I was now thinking "three quite serious incidents over these few years, perhaps I need a change of scenery?"

With that in mind and the fact that I had a growing family now whom I loved so dearly, I put in a written request for a change of Division which, with hindsight (if I knew then what I know now- that sort of thing), I should have remained on the Foxtrot Division where I knew what I was 'up against' (this will become all too clear later in).

And so, several months after my transfer request went through, I moved to the Lima Division.

CHAPTER SEVEN – 'L' DIVISION.

Initially I was based at a Police station just around the corner from the Foxtrot Division and it was just like being on the Foxtrot still because it was, after all, only two miles from there and so many of the crimes were caused by offenders from there which did have its advantages for me because I was able to put the knowledge I had gained to good effect and, if there was a 'thieves on' or a 'thieves disturbed' (where criminals were either breaking in to a property or had just made off), then I could use my local knowledge to plot which way they may take and in my first couple of weeks there, ended up crossing the Divisional border several times 'hunting' the criminals in their own back yard so to speak.

I bumped into some of my old colleagues from the Foxtrot regularly and they kept joking with me saying "see, you moved, but you just can't get enough of us can you Mitchell" which I found quite amusing.

I met my new Superintendent after a couple of weeks because he 'summonsed' me to his office to see how I was settling in and my response was "well sir, I asked for the Lima and got the Lima, but to be honest, where I am, I may as well have stayed on the Foxtrot".

Within six months, he had moved me to a place he described as a 'sleepy hollow', an old mining town and told me he wanted to see how I did there because it was a totally different way of policing and that it certainly was, with reasonable unemployment, crime beginning to increase and he seemed to 'take me under his wing', why I do not know, but one thing was for certain, I was going to show him what I was capable of.

The station itself was an old one which consisted of the old Police house connected to it which social services had bought and made their offices in and then the old station with cells from the Victorian era in but these were now used as locker rooms and a 'parade room' (where you started your duty and checked all the crimes from the previous day and did your report writing).

It was almost like an episode of 'heartbeat', like going back in time.

The Officers there were mostly 'old school' and were quick to inform me that they operated a 'fireman' shift (where they only went out if a call came in) and this just did not rest well with me because I was paid a good wage to do a good job which involved being out in the public view and not 'hiding away'.

The Sgt was also 'old school' but in a good way because he wanted Officers out on their beats patrolling and was very strict with that, the only downside to his 'vision' was that he only worked a day shift and so, as the old saying goes, when the cats away, the mice will play.

When he was around, Officers were out doing what they were supposed to be doing, or at least making it look like they were and when he was not, then, well old habits die hard so they say.

I was different, I would be out on foot patrol mostly, down footpaths, alley ways etc and this caused some upset with some Officers, but that was what I was paid to do and do it I would.

I had several 'face-offs' with older in service Officers but I stood my ground and told them "I am paid to do a job and that is what I will do, I am not bothered about what you want to do, just so long as, if I need help, then you are there for me because if you are not, then let it be said, YOU fired the first bullet".

One, Constable Daniels, decided to be extremely immature and began closing doors in my face, this was a grown man in his thirties who, I might add, had transferred from the Foxtrot Division only months before I started there and so I would have expected more of a professional attitude from him, but I later learned from a genuine colleague on his relief, that Constable Daniels had been the 'ring leader' in making trouble amongst the others about my attitude (of which I had none other than being honest and true as you have probably noted by now) and then it all fitted into place.

Anyway, I have never been the type of person to start trouble, but, if I am forced into a corner through no fault of my own, then I would come out fighting like a man possessed and take 'no prisoners' whether friend or foe and so, because of his stinking attitude, after 'passing off' several door slams by him, I took the bull by the horns so to speak and, in the rear yard of the Police station, went face to face with him after he had laughed and was about to slam the door again but MY FOOT prevented that!

No more than two feet between us I said "what is your problem?" to which Constable Daniels replied "You are because you're rocking the boat!"

He then followed up with "We DON'T go out on nights or afternoons, unless called and that has been the way long before you came".

I replied "well, if you want to sit on your lazy ass doing nothing and getting paid good money for it, then that is your call but I do not and if you continue in your ways and that puts me at risk, then believe me, ALL HELL WILL BREAK LOOSE".

This brought memories back of my first few months on the Foxtrot but I'd stood tall then and I was certainly NOT going to back down now!

Constable Daniels then made a move closer to me and so, instinctively, I moved back, clenched my fists ready to defend by attack and I make no apologies for this, I said "Do your worst now big man and it had better be good because you will only get one chance and I will take you down and won't stop, so GO AHEAD!"

Like all 'bullies' for want of a better word, because that is all he was trying to be, a bully, he saw that I meant business and how angry and 'hyped up' that I was and, after a couple of minutes of nothing, he backed down, no surprise there then!

Unbeknown to me, some of the other Constables had been watching through a 'mirrored' window (that allows you to see out, but not see in) and were amazed at how I'd faced up to Constable Daniels, taking me to one side to inform me that no-one had EVER done that before!

I gained quite a lot of respect from the ones who had witnessed this and Constable Daniels 'ego' had been quashed, quite rightly so.

I have said this before and nothing has changed in that I am a firm believer in 'karma' and all that goes with it.....if you do good and are a good person, then goodness will come back to you but if, however, you are a bad person, evil in some cases, then you've only got yourself to blame when you 'reap what you sow'.

I have seen 'bad karma' come to those who deserved it which I will touch upon later.

I did see a little 'Karma' in the case of Constable Daniels later in my career after I had been promoted when we had been called to a 'thieves disturbed' at a school premises and, by this time Constable Daniels was a Police dog handler and attended the scene.

His attitude had not changed whatsoever in relation to his laziness and being a dog handler only 'feathered his nest' in that respect because, at that time, if they made an arrest, then another Officer would deal with it to release the handler back to patrol and so, for a lazy Officer, this was their 'rainbows end'.

Do not get me wrong, these are the exception to the rule and the majority of dog handlers that I have worked with have been hard workers who would volunteer to assist in processing their prisoners, but Constable Daniels remained outside that.

So, on this call, I decided that I would ensure he earned his pay because his immediate summing up of the incident was "it's not worth getting the dog out, they will be long gone!"

Well, that may have been accepted by others, but not me because I knew that 'Leopards don't change their spots' and this was true in his case and so I gave him a direct order that I wanted the WHOLE premises and perimeter searched by him and his dog to ensure that the offenders had gone.

At the time it was raining and Constable Daniels said "Sarge, that will take a couple of hours and I may be needed elsewhere", which was a viable response if the Officer was genuine, but I felt different , knowing what he was like, and so I said "it's alright, if you are needed elsewhere, then I will make the decision whether or not to release you from this job" and then added to that "I'll wait here for your report back, just in case you get into trouble!"

It then started to rain heavily and let's just say that, whilst I waited in my dry Police vehicle, Constable Daniels got very, very, wet indeed, BUT, he got the message loud and clear!

Back to the old mining town and my work. I carried on Policing how I felt is should be done and, within six to twelve months, was offered (more like ordered really) via the Sgt but from the Superintendent, the role of Area Constable (community beat officer as they are now referred to) for another small community which definitely was like the sixties based Police series 'heartbeat' because this was made up of domestic dwellings and plenty of farmers and fields around.

This role also came with the use of a Police liveried (signed) motorcycle which I referred to as the 'Noddy' bike (from the very old children's characters Noddy and Big Ears for those who, like me, remember watching them as a child) because it only had a 125cc engine initially and had the full regalia of a proper traffic motorcycle apart from any sirens and so I, being 6' 4" tall, looked a little silly on it because my knees were almost past the front faring!

This got a little better when it was updated to a 250cc Yamaha and so was a little bigger for me.

I was told that the previous retired area Constable had done little to gain confidence from the public and I was to 'suck it and see' (a favourite phrase used by my Superintendent of that time) which meant, try it and if you like it and are successful, then stay and if you don't or aren't (successful), then come away.

This was a dream for me come true and I certainly was not going to let those who meant the most to me, the public, down and so I made a 'strategy' to 'prove myself' and gain the respect and support of the public which was:-

- Look at all the old 'home-watch' schemes and visit all the coordinators with a view to making them all fresh and effective again (something which was extremely neglected by my predecessor from the feedback I got) and give them all my direct contact numbers as well as getting theirs. I ensured that there was a meeting for 'home-watch' at least once every three months called by me or sooner should they request it and I got all the scheme coordinators to swap contact numbers and communicate with each other if something suspicious happened (home-watch is where neighbours keep a look out on their streets and contact the Police if something isn't right and in return, they would have a good community Constable keeping in touch with them whenever they were on duty).

- Visit all the schools from Infant up to Comprehensive and introduce myself to all the heads and teachers and then put in place a strong liaison plan which involved all pupils with films (Police related) for the Comprehensive students, cartoons and stickers for the Infants and Juniors on 'stranger danger' (to at least make them a little safer in changing times), and I also carried out (with written consent from all parents via the teachers) 'fingerprint for fun' classes where I would take fingerprints of the children as well as the teachers, on some 'fun sheets' that I had made for them to display in their classes and then, when the display was finished, they could take them home and all involved really enjoyed it! This was also a way to ensure that children WERE NOT AFRAID to talk to Police Officers, although there were a couple of families who refused to give permission (not unexpected because the parents were 'known' to me), so their children missed out on the fun and had to just sit and watch.

My heart went out to those few because, even though the parents may not like the Police, why should their children suffer, but they do say how the citizens of tomorrow grow up is down to their parents and, in my opinion, that is so true!

I also brought in 'mini uniforms' so that children aged between four and seven could 'dress up' in school like Police Officers.

- Visit ALL the farmers at their farms and check all their firearms and security for same which caused a little upset at first because I seized many, many guns from different farms (all legally held by them) until their security was up to that now required. It was quite frightening really where and how some of the farmers had previously kept their shotguns and ammunition because some were just 'under their beds' or 'in a kitchen cupboard', I joke not.

  Well that soon changed when I took over because, my view was simple, if these were not securely locked away in approved firearm lockers and fixed to solid walls with the ammunition kept safely again in approved secure boxes, then these could be used against innocent people by criminals or against the farmers themselves in a Burglary, or against myself or a colleague and so, after my initial few months sorting these out, I got the farmers back 'on-side' and they respected what had been done and most importantly, why I had done so.

I even 'closed down' a re-arming factory for illegal guns and this came purely by chance when I was checking legitimate firearms held and noticed several others hung on walls that had been deactivated (this is where the firearm is sent to a special place to be prevented from being fired usually by the barrel being filled with molten metal or the firing mechanism being removed and it is then certified as deactivated and can be held , providing it has a certificate from the premises that deactivated it because effectively, it is then just a piece of metal that looks like a gun), but these COULD be reactivated by re-drilling the barrel or making a 'replica' firing mechanism that works.

I fed this person a line that I was interested in these and we began chatting 'friendly' about the other weapons and also about the lawful 'reloading' facility (where the holder of a firearms certificate can in fact make their own ammunition, bullets and the like quite legitimately, providing they did not hold in excess of the amount allowed on their certificate).

I gained a lot of useful information that day, which, several months later, I was to fall back on when I was 'visited' by men and women in black!

These were from a special 'hush hush' unit dealing with illegal firearms in the city and the suppliers of same and, quite to my shock, this person was 'in their sights' and so I was 'interrogated', for want of a better word because they would only tell me that they asked the questions and I gave the answers!

We were ALL supposed to be on the same side, fighting crime, but I felt they saw me as somewhat of a 'pawn' or 'cavalry' soldier in a bigger 'war' and so, I gave them as much information as I could about what I had seen and the deactivated weapons in that persons possession.

It was suspected that they had been supplying reactivated weapons to criminals and utilising their 'reloading' facilities to do same reactivations, although I never did find out just how useful my information had been because one of their number would probably have taken all the credit for this.

I wasn't concerned because if, having supplied all the information that I had, the streets had been made a little safer, then lives would most certainly have been saved and that was all that mattered to me, my job was done.

- Re-open an old 'disused' police station to allow me to have 'surgeries' on my beat with my community but this took some 'haggling' to get permission from my Superintendent because it would involve spending quite a substantial amount of money on it to make it 'functional' for me, but I won the battle for that because I told him that all I needed was a roof that did not leak, a coat of paint for the outside and the notice board and not to forget the most important thing, a kettle and some cups- well, I would have to offer a cuppa to my community now wouldn't I?

So that was that, not a very difficult task to do and I found great appreciation coming from the community about what a difference I had made in such a short period of time, in fact, I had one streets residents write a major letter of 15 plus pages to the then Chief Constable about how I had solved a major problem with youths near to a High School that had caused them so much stress and duress when the previous community Constable had failed to act and I simply did it by hiding in bushes and witnessing, first hand, the actions of these youths and their anti social behaviour and then calling up two vans and 'front and backing' the alley they congregated in, then taking them all home one by one and telling the parents what their 'little angels' had done.

They could not argue because, after all, I had WITNESSED IT.

I then gave them a choice, they could do what parents should do and 'reign their kids in' or come to the Police station and act as 'appropriate adult' when I had charged them with offences that I had witnessed which included criminal damage, urinating, litter and public order (shouting and swearing etc).

Needless to say, the problem NEVER raised its ugly head again and quality of life for residents was given back to them by purely 'putting in the hours' to protect them. This problem had been ongoing for over three years and I stopped it completely in just one weekend with some good 'old fashioned policing'.

Being a community Policeman was a time that I can say I really enjoyed in my career because I could see, on a daily basis, the difference in the lives of people and their children and they would always approach me, the adults to thank me and the children to 'tax' me of any stickers that I had because I would always carry 'fun stickers' in my pockets or even in my helmet for any children that wanted them and the parents loved to see a Police Officer who was 'making the difference' and breaking down boundaries that had previously existed.

Together with a newly formed 'residents association' which I had helped to begin, we even managed to obtain a complete 'play area' and its equipment which had been destined for another area, but we found out that this had been cancelled and the equipment was going to be stored away because it wasn't needed so we took the bull by the horns, I from the Police perspective that this would give the youth somewhere 'controlled' to congregate and somewhere for the younger children to play thus reducing anti social behaviour and crime, and the residents from their perspective that the field where it could be located was being used to 'fly-tip'(dump rubbish) on and was dangerous for children and, together, we made it happen and to my knowledge it still is there today, something that I am very proud of because it was the Police and local community working in harmony to make a better place and I did not care for praise from my 'bosses' about a good job well done, no, for me praise from the community I served was the most important thing and meant so much.

After I had been given the role of Area Constable, I faced yet another confrontation from within the ranks through no fault of my own.

Constable Midge was an officer with no more than six years in service and had been at the station for most, if not all, of that time and when the Area Constable role I was offered came vacant, for reasons unknown to me, he was under the impression that it was to be him who would take that role.

Well, I am sure that you can imagine, when I was given the post, Constable Midge was extremely upset but this was through no action of mine because, as far as I was concerned, the powers that be had made a decision about my career path and I had accepted that and had no idea whatsoever of any other officers being interested, until, that is, one day when I was minding my own business writing up reports in the parade room (old cell) at the nick.

I sensed someone was stood behind me to my left and when I looked up, I saw Constable Midge looking very sternly towards me and so I asked him if there was anything I could do for him.

Simple question that would normally receive a simple answer, but not this question, asked of this officer, on this occasion, no, what occurred next was, in my mind, quite funny, but, perhaps not in the mind of Constable Midge whom, until that time, had never met me and nor I him.

The scenario went like this:-

Constable Midge - "Are you Mitchell Spence?"

Me - "Yes, I don't think we've met have we?"

Constable Midge - "No we haven't, and perhaps you may not wish to meet me again"

Me – "Why is that then? I am at a loss as to why"

Constable Midge then leaned towards me as I sat and quite loudly said "That Area job was mine and you have got no fucking right taking it, you've only just come here so what the fuck do you think you are doing?"

This took me by surprise because he was all of 5'5" if that and for such a small man he had such a filthy, arrogant mouth and so I decided to set the record straight immediately and with some verbal force too!

As I stood up, I saw Constable Midge suddenly become smaller than when I had been sat down and he too, saw me growing taller, much taller and, by the expression on his face, I believe he had started to think that perhaps his outburst might not have been the best way to start a conversation with me!

The conversation then became one way, perhaps you can imagine that, and it was one way from me to Constable Midge in the following manner "I don't know who you think you are fucking talking to, but let me make myself completely clear to you, I was offered the post not knowing if anyone was interested or not and I was given this presumably because I, unlike others here, actually work for a fucking living, so I suggest that, unless you want me to get really fucking off my head with anger by your arrogant, shit attitude, that you fuck off out of here now and perhaps look at yourself and your obvious failings, one being communication skills, do I make myself entirely fucking clear?"

Constable Midge had gone very quiet, oh, and very pale, because here I was all 6'4" of me towering over him with a rather angry face and temperament because, to be quite honest with you, I was finding more and more 'bad eggs' in the Police and as we all know, bad eggs are rotten and make all the nice ones look bad too.

Needless to say, Constable Midge and I never really saw eye to eye whilst on the Lima Division probably because he avoided me like the plague!

Bad Karma hit Constable Midge two years later with an injury and he was forced to leave the job and find work elsewhere in 'civvy- Street'.

One of my most satisfying incidents whilst area Constable was when a church on my 'patch' was regularly having one of its graves desecrated.

I have many strong beliefs for what is and what is not acceptable as I have previously told you, but this now became a 'new' moral standard for me because, there is low and there is unthinkable low, which, to attack the last resting place of someone, I believe is, well, I just cannot find the words to describe how disgusting this action is!

The headstone was being scratched and paint poured on it, there was a beautiful wooden bench opposite the grave under a willow tree which was regularly being scratched and the brass 'memorial' plate on it was defaced and any flowers or other tributes to the persons memory were being uprooted, smashed and thrown across the footpaths, yet of all the graves in the church yard, this was the only one being attacked.

A young girl was laid to rest in this grave and she had been knocked over on a busy road and tragically died as a result of the incident, so this was the only place that her mother and step father could now come to talk to her and cherish the short sweet life that she had lived before being sadly taken from them.

Well, I had children of my own and I was going to do EVERYTHING within my powers to stop this from happening anymore so, off I went to see my

Sgt and we put together an 'operation' which would involve sitting in a church every evening until midnight using video surveillance until we found the culprit.

For the next 10 days I and another colleague sat in that church, in the dark, each on our own, waiting and watching.

It's quite funny really, but two grown men, both Police Officers, found that sitting in a church in total darkness can be 'unusual' to say the least and both decided that we could not have been 'men of the cloth' so to speak because, when there is nobody around, the alter seems to take on a 'life' of its own!

Although we were there for a reason, to video the grave and those who attended, if there was any noise inside the church, the camera was turned to video anything that may have been there because we both thought that, should there be any 'apparitions', nobody would believe us unless it was on tape.

Nights came and went and I had done most of these but, as 'sods law' dictates, on the evening I was off duty and my colleague was there, the offender turned up and commenced their ritual damage to the grave.

I am glad really that I was not on duty that night because I would have found it extremely hard to just 'sit back and record' when an offence was being committed, but that was what covert surveillance was all about, gather the evidence and then, at a later date, arrest the offender, but this act disgusted me right to the core and my emotions may have got the better of me resulting in my going out and arresting there and then, in effect, blowing cover and that should never be done!

So, initially, when I came back on duty, I was very disappointed not to have been present at the time, but, because I had arranged the operation, I was given the 'right' to arrest which I was really pleased with because it was on my beat and I wanted to know who had been so low to do this.

When I ascertained who it was, I was extremely saddened and surprised because the 'offender' was a grandmother in her 70's who attended the grave of her great granddaughter which was right next to the one being desecrated.

Her first act upon arriving there was to kick any flowers off the grave and throw anything else that was present, across the grave yard before returning to her great granddaughters plot to 'tidy' it up and place new flowers on it.

How could anyone show so much 'bitterness' and anger to one grave only then demonstrate compassion and sadness towards the other?

I was passionate about this and so expedited the identity and arrest of this lady, which, yet again, led to me being assaulted by another who was under extreme stress and I will explain.

I went to the home address of the lady and, at that time, her own granddaughter was present. I tried to explain to her why I was there and that the grandmother whom she worshipped, had done something that was unacceptable and that she had to be held accountable for that.

Well, before I got any further, I was slapped across my face and kicked in the leg by granddaughter who was extremely angry but also in tears, which I could totally understand and so I let it go and simply 'restrained' her until she had calmed down.

Then I explained about the video and that I would have to arrest her grandmother but would treat her fairly because I could see, call it 'gut instinct', that this elderly lady was not normally a nasty person and there must be a reason for her actions, to which the granddaughter accepted the fate to follow and asked if I would keep her updated, which I gave my word that I would.

So, in came the grandmother, under arrest, and I interviewed her on tape.

It transpired that she had never been in trouble with the Police, which I suspected, and she admitted the offences of damage on numerous occasions because she was very fond of her great granddaughter and had previously asked permission of the church authorities to 'glitz up' the grave and had been refused.

This elderly lady was therefore upset that someone else was allowed to do so when she was not, but she was not aware that the 'ruling' had only recently been changed to allow this and so, had she made the request again, it would have been granted , thus preventing another family suffering heartache as a result of her actions!

A Police caution was administered to this lady and she was genuinely 'remorseful' about her actions, even volunteering to make right what she had done, something which the aggrieved persons did not wish to occur, which I can understand and respect.

Since that time, which is over ten years ago, the grave has been left untouched by anyone other than those who visited to mourn and the damage has all been repaired and, despite my not being a Police Officer anymore, every time I pass that church yard, I look across at the grave site and smile, knowing that the family are now happy and that poor little girl can at last rest in peace!

That, to me, is making a difference at its best, wouldn't you agree?

I spent several years as an Area Constable and thoroughly enjoyed the role but the time came when I decided that it was time to move on because my focus now was upon career development and, for me, that was working towards the next rank and becoming a Police Sergeant.

I approached my Superintendent and explained how I felt, expecting that he would not want me to leave something which had proved very successful but, as I had expected, he was a genuine boss who had both your interests and those of the 'organisation' in mind, unlike bosses of today, well, up until I retired on ill health, who seemed solely interested in themselves and how they could 'prove' how good they were, which, if it meant 'disciplining' others for minor matters, then they would.

So my Superintendent gave me his decision which was that he had been impressed at how I had 'turned around' the area and he wanted me to do the same with the other 'failing' area.

I was told that if I took the role of Area Constable for the other area, then he would, within six to twelve months, put me forward to go 'acting' (where you are a Sergeant and wear the three stripes on your uniform, but are 'observed' by an Inspector for anything between three to twelve months and 'reported back' on as to how you coped in the next rank. It was a 'temporary' rank, but as far as anyone was concerned, you 'walked the walk and talked the talk' and the decisions you made concerning Police-work were yours and yours only so, if they were good, you did well, but, if they were bad, then you took sole responsibility and 'carried the can' for them.

To become promoted, there was a very large amount of work you had to put in, of which the 'acting' was only a small part because, even after you had passed the promotional exam as I had, then you still had reports about you, assessment centres to attend, a promotional board to pass (where you were interviewed usually by three high ranking officers) and then sometimes a very long wait until you were officially promoted to the rank as substantive (confirmed as a Sgt).

And so, I took up his 'challenge', well, I could do nothing else really because had I refused, then I would have lacked one of the 'qualities' required, but deep inside, I knew that this was going to be an extremely difficult nut to crack.

After several months, I felt that this challenge had got the better of me and so, cap in hand, I went to see my Superintendent and explained how I had 'failed' in this role, but the reception I got was totally different to what I had expected because he explained that I had taken on board what he described as 'a very difficult role' and he had expected nothing less because apparently the residents did not seem to want a local Area Constable and that if I could not succeed to 'turn them around' as I had done with my first Area, then they could have their wish and he would not be placing another Area Constable there for the foreseeable future.

I was extremely relieved by this because I had felt like a total failure after my past success and my morale was suffering because of this, but my Superintendent and his comments 'lifted my spirits' back to where they should have been and he was, in fact, paying me a very high complement indeed which he followed up with a promise that I would be 'Acting Sergeant' at another Police station in the following few weeks.

CHAPTER EIGHT – ACTING SERGEANT DUTY.

I always remember the first tour of duty (T.O.D.) as an 'Acting Sergeant' because, when I walked through the station confines, a Constable, young in service, called over to me "Good evening Sergeant" and I totally ignored him, not because I was being ignorant because that was never in my character, but simply because, in my mind, I was still Constable Spence, and it took another call from the Officer to make me realise that it was me, I was the Sergeant that he was speaking to, Oh my god, and then I saw the three stripes on the arms of my tunic and laughed at myself and then turned around and apologised for not responding to him explaining that I was in a 'world of my own' at that precise moment, and I was because for me, there was no sergeant to ask advice from, I WAS THAT SERGEANT!

My new Police station was similar to where I had come from in its build design, the difference being that the Constables working there were decent 'coppers' and had no big 'egos' or laziness within them, they went out on patrol and did their job to the very best of their abilities and I respected them for that and, very, very quickly, they respected me which was half the 'battle' won when you were an acting Sergeant because the Officers you supervised could either 'make or break' you by being difficult to supervise or by being 'professionals' and these were most definitely the latter.

My time passed very quickly and I was a little upset when I had to leave the staff and return to Constable rank at another new station for me, but the time I had had was a very good experience with several 'characters' in the group who made it 'fun' to be there.

One occasion, when we were on night shift, a call was received concerning a 'disturbance' at a local public house and on this occasion, the staff I had were all engaged with persons they had arrested and so the area was left to be 'Policed' by myself and a 'Special Constable' (volunteers who have the same powers as the Police when in uniform but only in the area that they had been posted to) and so we went to look at the situation and assess what action to take, all two of us!

Upon arrival, I could see that several windows of the public house had been smashed and so I radioed in that this was a genuine call and asked for 'back up' from a T.A.G. (tactical aid group) patrol (now renamed to Tactical Aid Unit-T.A.U. because T.A.G. was deemed too aggressive!) whom I knew were on our Division that night and amongst them was a very honest, genuine and, well just decent Constable whom I will refer to as Constable Smyth.

I then entered the premises to find total carnage, windows smashed, mirrors behind the bar smashed and glass and broken chairs on the floor!

When I spoke to the Licensee, a lovely lady, she informed me that there had been a fight between five or six males, some of whom had now left, but several of whom were still in and she pointed to a male, in his twenties, who had a 'plaster cast' on his arm (presumably from previous fighting) who was sat down drinking his beer with others, but 'eyeballing' me as I approached.

I thought to myself "there are two of us, one of you, and in any case, you have a plaster cast on your arm so we'll go and see how the land lies".

This was a BIG mistake because as we approached him, he and two others stood up and shouted abuse towards myself and the Special Constable and then, the male in the 'cast' picked up a chair and threw it at us as others threw glasses and so, quite understandably, I made the decision to get the hell out of there and find out where my back up was!

The Licensee looked visibly shocked at our 'withdrawal' but, as I left, I shouted to her in the words, but not style, of 'Arnold Schwarzenegger, "I'LL BE BACK!"

Outside the public house, much to my relief, the T.A.G. (T.A.U.) patrol had just rolled up and my friend and colleague, Constable Smythe, described what he saw as something out of a 'wild-west' movie, which made me laugh.

Constable Smythe was such a 'placid' Officer and genuine nice human being, yet he was a very, very good wrestler and was on the Force wrestling team, so you would not want to get on the wrong side of him because appearances can, and in his case, are DECEIVING.

So, we went in, the Special Constable and I first and immediately the trouble group stood up and started shouting abuse again, to which I approached them and said "Have you met my mates?" and seven HUGE Constables entered behind me.

The faces of the offenders seemed to look concerned, well I would be if I were they, but that did not stop them and glasses started flying, tables were overturned and, well, it was carnage, but we got stuck in and made arrests, however whilst I was fighting with a male on the floor, I felt my foot and leg being twisted and it was painful so I looked around to see the next offender who I believed was attacking me whilst I made an arrest, only to find the Special Constable trying to 'rip my leg off', talk about 'friendly fire'!

I screamed at him to let go and, when he had calmed down a little, he realised his mistake and released his grip (I think he had a case of the 'red-mist' I have previously described which was understandable because I believe that this was his first 'piece of action' he had been involved in, poor fella).

We made several arrests and then processed them into the criminal justice system to appear before the courts and as far as I know, they pleaded 'guilty' to all charges and were all given heavy fines and had to pay compensation to the Licensee (quite rightly too).

Later on in my career, Constable Smythe contacted me and was obviously concerned because the 'Internal Investigations' had accused him of using 'unnecessary force' against the male in the plaster cast and 'failing to restrain him correctly with the speed-cuffs' we were issued with and were placing him before the Chief Constable for 'gross-misconduct' for which he, the most gentle and professional Police Officer I had ever known, could be sacked!

Obviously, I said immediately that I would be there for him, as he was for me on that night, and tell the 'internal investigations' EXACTLY what happened that night, which I did and was surprised to find that the 'crux' of their proceedings were based on the fact that the male who had his wrist and arm in plaster, had not had this hand cuffed and so, whilst trying to release his other 'cuffed' wrist in the rear of the van from the fixed bench on the floor, he had 'badly sprained' it and thus, made a complaint which the investigators had gone for.

When you read how I have been treated later in this book, the way in which Constable Smythe was being dealt with will be of no surprise you.

This was disgusting, the male could not have both wrists hand-cuffed because of his plaster cast and Constable Smythe did the best possible thing in the circumstances with a violent man and 'cuffed' his good wrist to the solid bench legs so that he could do no more harm to anyone else, I would have done the same and when I was 'interviewed' about this, I made it known that I felt they were being extremely stupid with their investigating him and then discovered that 'Internal Investigations' had 'overlooked' the most essential piece of 'evidence', the fact that this male HAD A PLASTER CAST ON HIS OTHER WRIST!

Needless to say, the matter was eventually dropped because I was prepared to call their investigations poor in quality and that a 'nursery' school- child could have done much better in my opinion in front of the

Chief Constable because I was really sickened that they were so 'gung-ho' on prosecuting Constable Smythe, that none of them had realised the practicalities of hand-cuffing a male in a plaster cast, it just CANNOT BE DONE.

Two officers whom I supervised whilst 'Acting Sergeant' always made me laugh because of the way they decided who would 'deal' with any job that they were allocated, by the flip of a coin!

It 'worked' for them and so I was not going to change something that worked, no matter how unusual it may be.

I shall always remember one night when we were called to a 'house party' that had spilled out into the street where disorder had occurred and, in itself, that was nothing unusual but, this night, things were to be so different as we soon discovered.

Upon arrival, there was a 'star-burst' where people just disappeared and we didn't know why until, that was, we went down the side path of the address and saw, a body!

Fortunately, the person on the floor was still alive but, quite shockingly, next to them was a loaded shotgun and so the matter became a very, very serious one indeed and I called up for the Inspector and C.I.D. to attend the scene.

Because of the 'clientele' in the immediate location (quite a few from the inner city area where crime and firearm shootings were rife, we immediately decided that the shotgun had to be moved and disarmed as I am sure you can appreciate to prevent someone drunk picking it up and god forbid, firing the weapon and so that was done straight away (which went against Force procedures somewhat because you should have called for an armed response vehicle, A.R.V. to attend so that the Firearms Officers could 'make safe' the weapon but we didn't have the 'luxury' of time or safe circumstances at that moment and so 'did what we did').

Once we had done this and placed it inside a locked Police vehicle, we could then treat the person on the floor whom we believed, at that time, had been an 'innocent victim', but our enquiries would reveal a sinister side to this in so much as this person had actually brought the shotgun to the scene and threatened to shoot the party-goers, thus, was knocked unconscious and had received quite a serious beating which could in no way whatsoever be shown to be in 'self-defence'.

The party-goers had 'dissolved' into thin air literally which we could not prevent because there were only four of us who attended initially so this left us with the occupants of the address where the party had been and they were not helping with identities of those responsible for the beating and the injured person who, as it turned out, was a school-teacher and lived with their mother next door and they could not identify their 'attackers' either.

After securing the scene as best could be done and interviewing witnesses, or at least the occupants who couldn't really go anywhere, we ascertained that the shotgun was in fact, illegally held by this school-teacher and that this person had also thrown a boulder through the rear window of the address because the party was too loud.

Obviously, that was going to be their career over because we had an obligation, upon conviction, to disclose to the education authorities, what had occurred, after all, they would be dealing with children and had been shown, all be it under extreme duress, to be a somewhat dangerous character and most definitely no longer able to continue in their line of work and so that was that.

It was decided that we would have a 'scrum-down' at the Police station after finishing at the scene of the crime, to establish a 'bigger picture' and focus upon what offences, apart from the obvious ones, we would be dealing with and that was when the 'flip of the coin' occurred between these two officers whom I shall refer to as Constable Ben and Gerry!

The two of them were together and so one would have to deal throughout and neither of them really wanted to because it wasn't exactly a straightforward matter and would take great expertise and patience to unravel, but Ben and Gerry were confident in the flip of the coin to decide because that is what they always did and so Ben flipped the coin and Gerry called heads or tails which he chose tails.

The coin spun through the air and both officers watched it like birds of prey, you could almost sense the sweat running off them because NEITHER wanted this call, but one of them would lose and as such have to deal and they both knew that this would test their experience in investigation and interview to the limit!

Down came the coin and bounced on the floor, rolling along the corridor, closely followed by Constables' Ben and Gerry until it came to a halt and fell flat!

The coin landed on HEADS and Constable Gerry looked shocked whilst Constable Ben had a 'Cheshire - cat' smile on his face (Big and beaming)!

Well, you would think that that was the end of it, Ben had 'won' and Gerry had 'lost' thus Gerry was dealing, but it was not because after the result, Constable Gerry looked at me, then at Ben, then at our Inspector who had come back to the station with us and said "So................what does that mean then? Do you want to deal with the job or shall I?"

Well, we all looked at each other and burst out laughing because Constable Gerry looked like a little child who had just had his favourite sweets taken from him and was about to burst into tears (he wasn't by the way, but that was how he looked) and, DESPITE losing the 'flip', was still trying to get Constable Ben to deal!

I know you may be thinking that this was a somewhat unprofessional way to deal with such a serious incident, but, I have to make it clear, all

Officers present had dealt with everything as professionally and safely as possible in the circumstances and this was a 'coping' mechanism of which Police Officers have many, to make light of such a matter and relieve the stress it causes.

It did not, at the time, or after on the follow up investigation, cause unprofessionalism or affect the outcome whatsoever, it was just human beings 'letting off steam' and I kept reminding Constable Gerry of that night right up until a couple of months before I left my career and retired!

I spend eight months as an Acting Sergeant and when I returned to the rank of Constable, nothing was the same because I had now experienced life as a Sergeant and knew totally, that this was where I wanted to be, a substantive Sergeant.

I had been given an excellent 'report' of how I had been by my Inspector whom I shall refer to as Inspector Rathbone and he had stated that I had many character traits required for the next rank and I was a Sgt who led from the front (well I believed strongly in the fact that, if you weren't prepared to do something yourself, then how could you honestly expect others to do the same and I gained respect for that view from the Constables I had worked with).

Respect is something you do NOT get as a 'right', you have to EARN although I came across many 'bosses' on the Lima Division who felt that it was their right because of the 'rank' they held and I would never be on their 'Christmas card list' so to speak because they knew how I felt on that score.

I was also driven by the fact that I had served under many Sergeants and, to be quite honest, I felt that they were not worth the pay they were given and I knew I could do a much better job.

I knew that, as a Constable, you can make a difference to the public by the way you dealt with your incidents however, as a Sergeant, you could make that difference considerably better because you could drive your 'visions' through your team and thus one voice could become seven or eight and that was my intention no matter how long or hard this would be, to give the public the service that they deserved, to make a difference for the better.

After twelve years in the rank of Constable, I was promoted to the rank of substantive Sergeant and my first 'posting' was a Police station on the Alpha Division.

CHAPTER NINE – 'A' DIVISION.

So here I was, 1995, aged 28 years and a Sergeant on the busiest Division, the city, facing 21 Constables at my first 'parade', all looking at me to give instructions to them regarding their duty beats, crimes, actions to be undertaken etc and believe me, I had never been used to having so many Officers on a relief, ever!

This was because the Alpha Division had been subjected to a process known as 'rationalisation' which is to make a company ,process or industry more efficient, especially by dispensing with superfluous personnel or equipment.

In common 'layman' terms this meant that all operational staff from three Police stations had now been relocated, together with their vehicles, radios and all necessary equipment, to one, hence there now being 21 constables on a parade when, previously, there may have been eight here, four at another station and nine at another.

This, rationalisation, in my opinion, was a 'figure fiddling' exercise whereby the 'powers that be' could now make it known publicly, that such a large number of staff were available for deployment and thus 'fool' or 'deceive' the public into believing that the streets were a 'safer place to be' because it looked as though there were more Police Officers available to 'fight crime' whereas in reality, the outer stations still had to be Policed yet now the Constables Policing them, had to travel from further afield.

I did not believe in deceptions like this then and still do not now, because, as I will explain at a later stage, this process continued until my retiring and, as far as I am aware, still does today with even fewer Officers available to be 'stretched'.

I found that I was one of three sergeants to supervise these officers, but, as time passed, this became one of two due to 'cut backs' and thus the work-loads increased for me and the other remaining sergeant because we were now two, doing the work for three.

The Police Federation of England and Wales up to December 2014, had disclosed publicly the figures of how many officers had been lost due to budget cuts by the Government under their 'austerity measures' and this was also widely reported in the national media.

Only recently, November 2016, they had circulated on social media, more concerns asking "what should Police Officers stop doing" This was connected to an article about the further cuts occurring in the fiscal year and the next, despite previously having been reassured by the Chancellor of the Exchequor that no further cuts would occur.

The concerning thing about this is that you, the general public, will most certainly suffer from these cuts because the 'thin blue line' is becoming even thinner and at 'breaking point'.

As is repeatedly reported, whilst these 'austerity measures' are in place, with public servants receiving a 1% or even less pay increase, the Government were still 'awarded' an 11% rise and always defended this by saying it was 'not their doing' and was awarded by an 'independent pay review system'.

It seems, in my opinion, that the Government are quick to change laws and procedures when they desire, but not when it suits!

The staffing levels of Constables, not surprisingly, also reduced by three if I remember correctly, thus only 18 covering the areas where previously 21 had stood which also increased the levels of stress upon the individuals and slowly but surely, over the months, a pattern was emerging of incidents 'piling up' to be allocated with no Constables available to deal and 'response times' increasing i.e. a call that should be answered and Officers dealing within 20 minutes, was now becoming 30-40 minutes if lucky.

My colleague and I both began patrolling on our own and dealing with any incidents that we could, to alleviate the pressures upon the other staff, despite this meaning that we were now interfering with our own roles and not having sufficient time to complete what was required of us holding the rank of Sergeant, but what could we do?

We couldn't 'magic' up another couple of Police Constables although we made plenty of paper cut-outs and handed them out on parades to try and 'lift' morale a little, making jokes about staffing levels and the like, but deep down, we knew that this was going to be the way of the future with Policing, and how right we were, disappointingly.

Recently, due to terrorist incidents, the Government announced that there would be more firearm officers patrolling the streets to prevent these but there is one question I ask which is this, where do these 'extra officers' come from?

The answer, from ordinary officers already serving and so, the operational numbers decrease again because firearm officers are 'specialist' roles and don't deal with 'normal' incidents.

Another question which is relevant when you read later in this book is this, how many officers will be prepared to carry the ultimate weapon of force for a police officer which can take a life in an instance, when they are already in a 'blame culture' that is now amongst the police?

I believe, in my opinion, very few indeed!

In an attempt to boost morale, we would take it in turns, on night shifts, to cook a 'curry' or a 'Chilli' at home before work and enough for all the staff we had and bring it in to be served up on refreshments periods (refs), however, there was many a time when it just went cold because nobody had had the chance to eat at their designated times or at all some nights and that, in itself, is a way of causing health problems such as diabetes or stomach ulcers later in life, but this was the way Policing was going (very similar to the Armed Forces now-so much pressure and work placed upon so few shoulders with so little resource)!

Demands continued to rise and resources continued to reduce and you would avoid at all costs, allowing a vehicle to be taken in for servicing, unless it was absolutely necessary because you knew that it would be 'off the road' for several days and this was because there was also a shortage in mechanics at the central garages, so there was many a time we would argue with the civilian supervisor at the garages about bringing vehicles in, unless we could either 'borrow' a 'pool car' (available to all the force) or have assurances that we could wait for the vehicle.

This was because it was actually more 'cost-effective' to lose an Officer from the strength whilst they waited for their patrol vehicle to be serviced, rather than dropping the vehicle off and losing it for days at a time when three or four Officers would then not have the means to do their job, because, despite having fewer vehicles at our call, we were not allowed to 'double-up' (two Officers patrolling together) because that would give the impression to the public that Officers on the streets were less, despite this becoming reality.

Even as of December 2014, when it was reported in the National media that West Midlands Police had disclosed a threat being received that a Police Officer could be taken hostage and killed, the 'doubling up' of Police Officers was still not allowed, yet Police Community Support Officers were allowed to do so.

My tours of duty would become longer because I, as did some of the other Sergeants as time went by, would come in earlier to prepare for the shift ahead and leave later, to catch up on things we had not been able to complete during our shift and this was making our 10 hour shifts become more like 14 when you put travelling to and from work into the equation because none of us lived where we worked, some even lived in Wales, YES, Wales and had to travel cross border!

Some Constables had also begun doing this and the strains were beginning to show because I remember attending an incident where a store security guard had detained a shoplifter but, in the process, he had been threatened with a knife and NONE OF THE CONSTABLES WANTED TO ARREST THE OFFENDER!

This was because they were 'fearful' of the paperwork involved and not being allowed the time to process, uninterrupted, the offender and these were Officers who had worked damned hard but were now feeling the effects of the 'rationalisation' and all that comes with it.

Eventually, I had no option but to give a direct order to one Officer to arrest the male and deal with it and then, later, address all the Officers involved quite sternly (but I understood their feelings and how this had occurred yet I had to make them know that it was totally unacceptable how events had rolled out on that occasion).

As far as bosses in the 'Chief Inspector' and above ranks were concerned, this was your 'relief' and you would manage them and all the trials and tribulations effectively to provide a 'service' to the people, despite it being those higher ranks that were, in my opinion, becoming 'puppets' for the political parties concerned and accepting harsh 'cutbacks' without argument, they were no longer in the 'real-world' of Policing a city centre streets with the volume of crime and serious incidents it had.

In fact overtime would have assisted in resolving the problems of staffing, yet it was like trying to squeeze blood out of a stone to obtain even the slightest amount of overtime when needed and yet, towards the end of each financial year in March, there was overtime being allocated for the most ridiculous of reasons so that it could be 'spent for the sake of spending it' because, if you did not utilise all the overtime budget up, then the next year, it would be decided that you didn't need the same amount as the previous year because it hadn't been spent and so it would be REDUCED!

There is a saying "mine is not to reason why, mine is just to do or die" and yet I was reasoning why all the bloody time because I could see that this, if allowed to continue in this way, would, eventually, in my opinion, be the 'self-destruct' button for the Police Force (or service as the Government departments like us to refer to it as) and if you look at the way the Police were in 2013, there was and still is to this date, 2016, most definitely a 'disaffection' towards Government 'brewing' and the Government, like so many before them, are totally ignoring the warning signs and sounds as the Police volcano begins to rumble.

This is also evident in the way that the Government are currently treating the Fire Service and NHS Junior Doctors which has and will continue to cause them to take Industrial action.

We all know the 'spin' placed upon the 'benefits' that the Police Officers have in relation to their 'gold-plated' pension final salary scheme, but let me tell you all this, here and now, for those Officers who are in that said scheme, they pay a very large amount of their wages into the funding of same, so why should they not be entitled to the benefits of it if, and I do say if, they manage to complete their 30 years service to the Crown without becoming disabled by a violent attack or worst still, murdered by a criminal!

It is not very common knowledge that the Politicians are in a virtually identical scheme, however, the difference is that, as far as I am aware and this was from information that the Police Federation disclosed many years ago, they contribute very little into that ,no, it is paid to them as a 'right' for their services apparently.

That alone, causes a large amount of dissent within the Police Officers who are now, as at September 2016, being 'attacked' from all corners, from the Government, from Criminals and from a proportion of the members of the public who only know what they hear in the way of 'spin'.

I have said this before, Police Officers MUST be accountable and MUST NOT feel untouchable, but that does not mean attacking their families and standards of living because, mark my words, that WILL ONLY LEAD TO SERIOUS CORRUPTION and, as I will explain further along in this book, I have fought against corruption in many different forms on so many different occasions and if you pay a Police Officer poorly, then the 'temptations' will open to them to perhaps take on a second job (currently only allowed in certain circumstances) which could leave them open to 'blackmail' or worse-still, taking payments from 'dubious' characters for information (as has been shown in other countries where Officers are on criminals 'pay-rolls') and would you want to see that happening because I know I certainly would not, BUT, IT IS A POSSIBILITY, mark my words.

In December 2014, the Police Federation of England and Wales reported on social media sites and in the National Media, news that the Metropolitan Police in London, were looking at accepting people with 'minor' criminal convictions into the Police which, I am sure you will agree, is a somewhat 'dangerous' and 'risky' road to travel down.

I am certain that this is because the Police, as a career is no longer a prosperous and financially rewarding career considering the tasks required of Officers presently and the lack of 'respect for authority' in society today, together with the lack of appropriate sentencing being given by the courts to convicted offenders.

Even whilst I was on the Alpha Division, I had my suspicions that a Constable and possibly a Sergeant were 'on the take' (receiving something from the criminal fraternity indirectly) because they were always patrolling together and seemed extremely friendly with the prostitute community which was quite large around there and one weekend, I had suggested that we put together an operation to deal with the prostitution problem which also linked into other aspects such as 'quality of life' for residents, motorists being 'propositioned', 'pimps' attacking men who weren't interested and then also attacking their prostitutes if they weren't 'on the game' enough and so, an operation to 'make the Police presence known', would hopefully disrupt 'business' and, if successful, could be repeated as many times as required to solve or at least reduce the problem!

So, after observing 'the streets' for a couple of weeks, it was seen that each weekend was busy, but Saturdays seemed to be extremely 'intense' for prostitution and so I put together an 'operation' which was given the approval to go ahead the following weekend.

Both the Sergeant and Constable were extremely interested in participating in the operation and it was felt by the bosses that they had valuable intelligence to offer and so, when the time came, they were 'involved'.

On the Friday night, the streets were full of prostitutes 'plying' for trade, yet on the next night, the date of the operation, there was not one prostitute to be found on the streets in question whatsoever.

Somebody 'in the know' had tipped them off and, although I could not prove who it or they were, I, together with others, had a very good idea and this illustrates my previous concerns concerning the Metropolitan Police considering 'minor convictions' being 'swayed in order to recruit.

And what would their rewards be for doing this, I shudder to think about the answer to that question.

I am sure that I do not have to suggest any, especially as later on, between 2000 and present (the exact dates I am uncertain of), Police Officers have been convicted of Indecent assault and Rape whilst on duty and in their patrol vehicles and, if I am not incorrect, a Constable was also convicted of indecent assault with a prostitute or drug abuser who was under arrest and 'in custody' at a Police Station and was forced to perform 'oral sex' with them in the cell. Only in December 2016, the media reported that approximately 300 Police Officers either have or are being investigated for abusing their position to obtain sexual favours.

All of which were reported on in the National news and papers, so you can probably see where I am coming from on this can't you?

I have always and still do, believe that a Police Officer should be an 'exemplary' citizen who has no criminal record or criminal cautions whatsoever, yet one of the Officers I referred to above had previously been in trouble with the Police prior to their joining up and had been cautioned for stealing a motor vehicle!

The rehabilitation of offenders act is there in statute to allow people with criminal convictions that are 10 years or more past, to have a 'second chance' in life with employment etc and I agree, in principal, with that, but not for occupations such as the Police, Armed Forces or similar where there is access to very, very sensitive material, records or weapons and there is an extremely high 'trust' placed upon the individual because, as can be seen from my explanation above, the trust, on this occasion, was abused, so what other things had this or these two Police Officers done and 'got away with'?

I always remember an incident, which I never told my wife about for many years until one evening, after I had had a few drinks and was chatting to some friends of ours, not knowing that, as I was in 'full flow' of recollecting this, my wife was stood behind me and it all came out.

It wasn't because anything wrong had happened that I didn't tell her, it was because, in my own way, I was protecting her from the harsh 'realities' that I faced whilst policing the Alpha Division and I did not want her worrying about me (not that she didn't anyway because what 'spouse' wouldn't worry) when a Police Officer went to work?

This incident was one I will NEVER forget and one for which I have had many a disturbed night sleep over since, especially when you recall the fatal shootings of those two young and, in my opinion, very brave policewomen in 2012.

The afternoon was a normal, if any could be normal, shift when a call was received regarding an 'armed robbery' that had 'gone wrong' somewhat for the offender concerned and they had made off from the scene in possession of what appeared, from witness accounts, to be a hand gun (firearm).

Information was received regarding a male who potentially fitted the description of the offender, having been seen to go into an address and so we got the call to investigate.

Obviously, other Officers attended the immediate scene, but, were very reluctant to 'knock-on' the address (see if anybody was in by knocking at the door)!

These Officers were 'young in service' and, when I attended, appeared somewhat frightened (understandably) and so I took control and requested the A.R.V. (Armed Response Vehicle) to attend together with some more Officers.

As a Sgt, I was not supposed to be 'first' because my role was to 'effectively supervise, guide and direct' other Constables, but, on this occasion, I had to put my own personal views before that of what should be done and it could have quite easily cost me my life.

At that time, an UNARMED officer would have to do the 'knock-on' even if A.R.V. were present and the Armed Response officers could not 'self-arm' without authority from a high ranking officer (I think, if I am not mistaken, that this could be a Chief Superintendent initially but it then had to be 'ratified' or 'rescinded' by an A.C.C. - Assistant Chief Constable, as soon as was possible afterwards and, as you can possibly imagine, a lot can happen between an UNARMED officer facing a firearm and such 'authorities' being issued and so we 'had a little chat', the Armed Response Officers and I did!

Because the officers at the scene were 'apprehensive', I decided that I would go and 'knock-on', with the understanding from A.R.V. that they would be hidden around the side of nearby hedges, WITH WEAPONS DRAWN, and, should the inevitable happen and a gun was seen, they would then show themselves and take control, which I respected very much because I knew that they were 'putting their own necks on the line' somewhat and expediting the matter of safety for me.

And so I approached the door of this address, looking through windows as best I could on my approach but to no avail, and then, looking back over my shoulder to ensure what was agreed was happening, gave the knock on the door, and waited for what seemed like forever.

I did feel afraid, after all, the circumstances would have made anyone afraid, knowing they may be about to face a gun wouldn't they?

A short while later, the front door opened and I was met by a male with his arms behind his back with a greeting of "what the fuck do you want?"

I responded and explained why I was at his address because a male fitting the description of an offender with a gun, had been seen entering, I believed, this address and the male then responded with "Fuck off, there is nobody here but me so just fuck off!"

After a few seconds I then put to this him that he, in fact, fitted the description of the male and did he have a firearm of any sort whatsoever, because, after all, it could have been an air pistol too.

The male then moved his arms from behind his back and brought them around towards me, WITH A PISTOL IN HIS RIGHT HAND and pointing it towards me shouted "Do you mean this fucking gun?"

I was now looking down the barrel of the gun and the fear and sickness I felt at that exact moment in time was indescribable, my legs went all 'wobbly' and I just thought "SHIT!"

I was extremely relieved as the Armed Response Officers made themselves known and shouted, guns pointing, something like "Armed Police, put your weapon down and your hands on your head, NOW!"

Well, obviously, I moved aside and allowed them to 'take the lead' and my 'young' colleagues were shocked, but the offender was compliant and even joked "it's just a fucking starter pistol!"

This matter was dealt with by C.I.D. and I do not know what the outcome was, I presume a 'guilty' plea because I never had to go to court for it, I was just glad to be alive, hence why I never told my wife for many, many years and only because I had got a little drunk.

Procedures have changed extensively now and A.R.V. Officers are permitted, I understand, to 'self-arm' as and when required because firearm incidents have become somewhat more frequent as the years have passed.

As a Sergeant, no matter how experienced or inexperienced you are, you are looked upon by your staff as the 'font of all knowledge' because, after all, you have passed your exams and the promotional system and so, should know 'everything' and have dealt with everything which is not always the case, well, how could it be because there are always incidents that are new to even the most experienced officers and the next situation is one that will stay with me forever because it was so very close to my heart.

A female Constable, whom I shall refer to as constable Jennings, was sent to a 'cot death' whilst very young both in service and age and, quite correctly, called upon me for help.

I arrived at the scene to be met by her, close to tears, and a young 'mum and dad' who were hysterical because their little baby girl had been found by them dead.

In a situation like this there are many thoughts going through your mind namely that you have a 'sudden death' of such a delicate nature, a family destroyed with anguish and grief, an Officer obviously distressed and a potential 'crime scene' and so you have to be very, very professional yet caring and considerate and, believe me, having a young family myself at that time, dealing with something like this and attempting to keep my own emotions out of view, it was very difficult and stressful for me, yet I was the one whom everyone concerned was looking to for help!

I will never forget the image inside my head because of this and have dreamt about it on many occasions.

The little girl was no more than eight months old and looked like a 'wax model' lying there in her cot with no life, still wrapped in her shawl and I had to pick that baby up and check her for any obvious signs of 'unnatural' causes i.e. injuries, bruising etc, whilst still being compassionate with the parents, ensuring that I did not 'disturb' any 'evidence' and by evidence I mean, bedding, clothing, feeding bottles, sterilising equipment etc because all this would have to be 'bagged and tagged' (evidence has to be dealt with in such a way, numerically listed with exhibit numbers and letters of the officer seizing i.e. M.S.1, 2, 3 etc).

I decided that the best way to deal was to sit the parents down after checking that life had been pronounced as extinct by the paramedics who attended and seizing the relevant paperwork results from those checks and explaining, with as much tenderness and understanding as I could, the process that must occur not only to ensure that the coroners' inquest proceeded correctly, but also so that the parents could be 'eliminated' from the enquiries and, in due course, be allowed to grieve for their daughter, something that I believe is an extremely important and necessary emotion with any bereavement and so that is exactly what I did, informing my 'comms' that I was at the address but that my radio would be switched off as a gesture of respect for the family whilst I was there and dealing together with Constable Jennings.

As far as I was now concerned, no other incident would take precedence at this time and, after some considerable time and explaining, the parents fully understood and assisted in the procedures that were to follow.

My own heart was aching because these parents were looking at me for support, yet were not much older than I and I found it extremely hard to keep a strong exterior on show to display I was 'in control' and would be there for them, when deep inside me, all I wanted to do was to cry because I could 'feel' their grief and emotions and also, as a parent myself, could picture myself in such a traumatic situation and believe me, that hurts like hell.

These are the type of incidents that the Police have to deal with that are so much from the normal duties carried out and, from my own personal experience, stay with you for life.

An 'ordinary' vocation it is not and this is why the pay should always reflect that fact.

I was to spend a couple of years on the Alpha Division and the latter part of that was as a Custody Sergeant.

I believe in 'innocent until proven guilty' and as a 'custodian' of persons accused of criminal offences, I would strive to ensure that they were treated correctly and in line with the legislation and 'codes of practice' for detained suspects.

Do not get me wrong, I was no soft touch and if detainees were violent etc, then 'reasonable force' would be used to ensure the safety not only of them, but also of my Officers and I and I would always be there to ensure that nobody was treated with 'excessive force'.

The Police Officers came to know that I was 'firm but fair' on all parties concerned and I would never allow professional standards to slip.

I was nicknamed 'Sergeant P.A.C.E' (because I knew my legislation extremely well and the Officers knew that if I did not have the answer, I would research and find it.

I did have a couple of 'disagreements' with other Custody Officers both here and on the Lima when they had authorised a persons' detention and when I came on, I released them without charge because there was insufficient evidence to detain them, let alone process them any further, but that was right and proper, after all, as I have said previously, we are there to uphold the law and not make or break it.

As Custody Officer, I did experience several 'attempt suicides' by detained people in custody and I would do everything to make them safe (Drs, hospital etc) and then submit a detailed report concerning the circumstances and action taken to the Superintendent to ensure that, should there be a query from the Media, then all the facts were fully reported and this was commented upon positively on several occasions.

There were some 'humorous' attempt suicides which were most definitely not serious and two that remain extremely clear in my mind were a man who tried to kill himself by 'holding his breath', no joking this was what he tried to do and for that one, I merely entered the facts upon the custody record but did treat him as 'vulnerable' and called for a police Dr to attend and check him over regarding his state of mind.

The other one that still 'amuses' me to this date was that done by a gentleman who did try to hang himself with a cord he had managed to rip out of his jogging bottoms.

The cord was tied, quite tightly, around his neck and when we came to his help in the cell, he was trying to ask us to get it off him because it had 'gone wrong' and was hurting him which I can understand because he had tied the other end to the drain in the centre of the floor!

Can you believe it, an attempt hanging, from the floor, strange, but true.

He had tied it, then leaned away from the drain to tighten it around his neck, but then decided that it hurt too much and was being 'throttled' but not enough to kill himself fortunately.

Again, I treated it as a 'serious' attempt and after releasing and treating him, he became a 'vulnerable' detainee and my report was submitted although I did get some comments made by other 'colleagues' but did not care, an attempt is an attempt no matter how 'weird' it may be.

CHAPTER TEN - RETURN TO THE 'L' DIVISION.

I decided that now I had had inner city experience as a Sgt, I would put a request for a transfer in to return back to the Lima Division because I wanted to 'change' the way Constables had been when I was there originally and give 'direction' for the better and so, in 1999, I returned and almost from day one, I faced a constant battle against corruption and rules that were being 'bent', something which did not sit comfortably with my beliefs.

Within a short period of time my Inspector retired and a newly promoted Inspector took his place, someone whom I shall refer to as Inspector Boddingley and believe me, there was no 'honeymoon period' with him because he was a very arrogant man who had the attitude of 'I am the boss and you will do as I say, even if I am wrong', well, I was not going to become a 'puppet' for anyone and if something was morally or criminally wrong, then I WOULD STAND UP AGAINST IT, no matter what the consequences were!

I became the Custody Officer for my relief, but was approached by other relief members (there were five reliefs A to E on the Lima Division who all had two or three Sergeants and an Inspector each) for advice on legislation and also situations that were occurring with their colleagues because my reputation for honesty and knowledge of the law had followed me and I was quite satisfied with that and took it as a complement.

On one of my first shifts with this man, I had an attempt suicide in my custody of which I had had numerous when I was a Sgt on the Alpha Division.

My normal procedure with this was to deal with the situation then 'bag' and 'tag' any 'evidence' and submit a full report to command to ensure that they were aware should there be any press enquiries.

I had only ever received praise from the Alpha Command for my dealings.

Inspector Boddingley, however, was different, trying to make a name for himself, and so he told me to seize the custody record when my relief came to take over from me, write that I had seized it upon the record and then go and see him which was not normal procedure, that was something that 'internal affairs' would do should they feel there were some 'inconsistencies' or 'lies' on the custody record and, as far as my duties and records were concerned, that would NEVER be the case.

I was treated as if I was a suspect by him and scrutinized well into my own time after my shift had finished.

Line by line I had to explain all the record and my actions and my Custody Sergeant colleagues even rang me at home to tell me that he even came in the following day (his day off) to go and see the Superintendent regarding this as if he was trying to prove something against me.

I spent the weekend worrying sick about why I was being treated differently to previous incidents in the city.

I could now see how my professional 'relationship' with Inspector Boddingley was going to roll out.

I reported a Sergeant who, in my opinion, was a 'corrupt' officer to Inspector Boddingley.

This was a Sgt whom I shall refer to as Sgt Tamar.

This Sgt, again newly promoted in the last 4 to 12 weeks, admitted to me that he was 'stitching' up a Constable whom I shall refer to as Constable Stephenson.

Sgt Tamar told me he was putting a report together which was a lie so that Constable Stephenson would be subjected to 'disciplinary action' because he did not like the Officer and he was going to say that the Officer had told Sgt Tamar to "Fuck off" and was refusing a lawful order.

I had worked with Constable Stephenson on many occasions at the Central Custodial Centre (C.C.C) on the Alpha Division and he was an exceptionally professional, polite and hard working Officer and so I was not going to stand by and allow such corrupt actions to occur.

I challenged Sgt Tamar and he said, "Prove it, I'll deny it, it's your word against mine!"

I told Sgt Tamar face to face that he was 'bent' and a disgrace to the uniform and badge that he wore and that it was corrupt cops like him that made other decent Officers face the 'hostilities' and 'distrust' that they do now.

I later learnt, from my own horrendous experiences of corruption and lies made by higher ranking Officers than I against me, that the only way you can be heard and believed is to openly record your conversations with them on voice recorders and, believe me, they become very 'by the book' because they know that voice recorders do not lie, (You will read more about that later in this book).

I went next door to Inspector Boddingley because I was totally disgusted by Sgt Tamar and his lies but was told, to my horror and disgust by the inspector "Sgt, go back to your Custody Office and deal with your custody matters, leave the outside Sergeants to deal with their staff, understood?"

I was given the 'cold shoulder' for being honest!

I later found out that Sgt Tamar knew Inspector Boddingley when he too was a Sgt and so the puzzle starts to fit together doesn't it?

Constable Stephenson was moved to another station as a result of Sgt Tamar and his lies but, if he was capable of this act of corruption, then what else was he capable of?

This was only the 'tip of the iceberg' where these two were concerned.

Inspector Boddingley would 'allow' 'misdemeanours' to occur in relation to a female Sgt whom I will refer to as Sgt Sykes who was also on our relief and who he had become 'extremely friendly' with in such ways as allowing 'extended' refreshment meal break periods so that she could be an instructor at PAID fitness classes at a local gym, based in an old warehouse.

This sort of thing was not allowed whatsoever unless you had applied in writing, to the Chief Constable and received approval because it was a second Income, classed as a 'Business Interest' and from enquiries I had made, this had never been done by Sgt Sykes, yet Inspector Boddingley was 'turning a blind eye' to this breach of procedures.

Obviously, I made representations about this because, on several occasions I had been called upon to give advice to 'comms' or Officers because neither he nor Sgt Sykes could be contacted and I was the Custody Sgt and in Inspector Boddingleys own words was to "go back to your Custody Office and deal with your custody matters, leave the outside Sergeants to deal with their staff, understood!"

Let's just say that when I made my representations known, Inspector Boddingley just 'smirked' and walked away.

Sgt Sykes is now a high ranking Officer, and I feel sick when I think about the 'close' relationship that they seemed to have, which had also been noticed by other Custody Sergeants too!

When someone is in custody suspected of committing an offence, they are subject to 'reviews' of their detention to ensure that their arrest and detention is lawful and still necessary.

These reviews are carried out by the 'duty Inspector' for someone who is not charged, but, in addition, after a certain period of time, a Superintendent must be contacted to 'extend' the detention further, should that be necessary, up to a maximum of twenty four hours, by which time the police MUST have applied to the courts for any longer detention.

These Superintendent reviews are IN ADDITION to any done by the duty Inspector and ALL Inspectors knew that, apart from Inspector Boddingley who seemed to make his own 'laws and procedures' up as he went along.

Inspector Boddingley refused to carry out a review of detention on a detainee after 9hours in custody when I asked him to, his rationale being that the Superintendent had already done her review and he was not required to do so.

This was a totally incorrect procedure and the detainee was in for MURDER, so a breach in procedure could result in the trial being brought into disrepute.

I prided myself on being by the book, honest and fair and so I was left with the choice of ringing the Superintendent up at 3am, but I respected them and did not wish to do this and so I suggested that I ring several other Custody Officers to voice their opinions even though I knew I was right.

Eventually, after my doing the telephone calls, the Inspector did what he was obliged to do, a review, BUT, wrote on the custody record that it was delayed due to 'operational reasons' which was a LIE!

I decided that I would wait until the trial for this matter and should I be called as a witness, then I would, on oath, fully explain what Inspector Boddingley had actually been doing which was SLEEPING!

Unfortunately, I was never called to court for any trial and can only presume that the offender had pleaded 'guilty' to the crime and so my 'day in court' never came.

Inspector Boddingley became extremely negative towards me because, I believe, he didn't like a meagre Sgt telling him his job, even though he was getting things wrong.

I subsequently had time off and annual leave requests refused without reasonable rationale, favouring the two other Sergeants before me.

The staff on my relief also took a dislike to him as did numerous Custody Sgt colleagues from other reliefs which illustrated that it was he who was causing great dissent.

I have always believed that if you fall out with one person over a matter, then that is 'normal' because you cannot always be of the same opinion, but, if you fall out with every person you meet or supervise, then you MUST look at yourself because that indicates something quite wrong indeed and this is what was occurring with Inspector Boddingley.

I regularly liaised with the law research department to back my views up because he would not take my advice and on one occasion, in the Custody Office, he was informing the then Superintendent, how he was right and I was wrong on a particular matter of law, which I had already had confirmed I was right and had a print out of the relevant legislation.

I allowed him to finish his speech to the Superintendent and then produced the paperwork and informed the Superintendent of my advice, his refusal to take same and that I was right.

This was not for 'brownie points' or anything else, merely that I took pride in my knowledge and doing the job right.

My role was made all the more 'difficult' because of my 'stance' although I had the full backing of all my colleagues and, over time, my health began to suffer although that was only the start of many, many battles that I was to face.

After constant 'attacks' by Inspector Boddingley, I went on holiday thinking it was just overwork causing me to feel tired, washed out, tearful and snappy with my family, however, after a refreshing break in Turkey, from day one back, I felt ill again.

All came to a head when I shouted at my then 8 year old child to "get off their fat lazy arse" so that I could get into the freezer!

Obviously they were upset and crying and I could not believe I had said that to a child, this was not like me and I went into my lounge and broke down in tears.

I will never forgive myself for that verbal attack upon them, whom, like all my family, I loved so very, very much and will 'take that to the grave' with me, despite their telling me on numerous occasions in the last five years or so, that they forgave me many years ago because I had been fighting so very hard against 'demons' in my head and that, to me, is the best way to describe my depression, anxiety and stress because you do fight, daily, with 'dark influences' that 'attack' your mental health and do cause you to behave irrationally.

Believe me; I have had suicidal thoughts and come so very close because of how I had been treated by 'the Police Family'.

You never recover from a depressive illness, you learn 'coping mechanisms' to help you each and every day, but sometimes you still succumb to the illness and that is when my family and close friends were 'on alert' to watch my demeanour and look for any 'warning signs', but you can manage, no matter how hard it feels.

An appointment was made for me to see my G.P. and when I did, I completely broke down and was told that I had severe Depression, Anxiety and Stress and was signed off work immediately with medication.

'Modern day Policing' had taken its toll upon me, but this was only the start of a TEN YEAR plus battle against mental illness and the varying forms of corruption within!

I wrote a poem about when you are low and called it 'Life's A Gift'.

When the world around you feels so blue,

And there's nothing more that you can do…

Just think of those you hold most dear,

They're there for you, to face your fear.

Look back at all the good that you are,

Push fear far away, push it oh so far.

If you weren't here, and left them all,

How would they feel, not tall but small.

They'd hurt themselves with thoughts of you,

And ask was there more that they could do?

Be strong and hold your head up high,

This rhyme comes from my heart,

So look up to the sky.

How would those close feel if you left this place?

A heavy loss to the Human Race.

No matter what life throws at you,

Be strong and talk because you WILL get through!

And when you look back in your future time,

You will be glad of the moment you took to read this rhyme.

CHAPTER ELEVEN – MENTAL ILLNESS AND THE POLICE.

The Police Force or Service as the politically correct like to refer to it, have a 'duty of care' towards its members as well as the public (or 'customers' as we were told to refer to them)

And, as far as mental illness was concerned, if you looked ok on the outside, then, as far as some organisational representatives were concerned, nothing was wrong with you and they would try to put you through 'disciplinary' regulations or 'efficiency' regulations rather than doing what they were supposed to do and give you help.

This was despite having an 'Occupational Health Unit' (O.H.U) with trained doctors and nurses as well as counselling services available to intervene at the earliest possible opportunity and try and 'fix' you before you became 'damaged beyond repair' so to speak.

As you will see from reading later on, some of the 'bosses' in my Force deemed themselves to be more knowledgeable in mental health than the paid experts and thus would go on to ignore the medical advice given, favouring their own actions instead which is quite shocking.

It was bad enough being a Constable and suffering because of the way you would be treated, but to be a Sergeant, as I was, and then to openly admit you suffered from mental illness, brought with it a cynical, stereotyping, oppressive and arrogant attitude towards you from Human Resource Civilians as well as your immediate 'Inspecting' ranks above you which, in turn, only caused your condition to worsen.

This was across the board, certainly on the Lima Division where I now was and the reluctance to help you in any way whatsoever was immense and you were paid 'lip service', nothing more and nothing less.

After my breakdown, I returned to work 6 months later due to the threat of half pay and came under the care of the occupational health nurse, together with Welfare, a counsellor and my own GP as well as the Force Medical Officer whom I shall refer to as Dr Slade and was given suitable duties with roll call to recuperate (Roll Call is where you organise resources, duties, leave rotas etc).

I had referred myself to the O.H.U because I knew that I wanted to recover and be able to get on with what I was being paid to do, but did not want to go anywhere near my previous Inspector Boddingley, whom, as far as I was concerned, was not, shall we say, the 'straightest' cop I knew.

I became involved in constructing and then supervising the Performance Management Unit on the Lima Division.

Performance had now become the 'big thing' in the Police and all Officers were required to meet specific and quite harsh 'targets' that would be scrutinised by 'Command' at Divisional level and then the Chief Constable at Force level and specific 'Performance Management Units were being put together to monitor these targets which, in my opinion, did not focus whatsoever on the 'broader picture' of what Officers were actually doing whilst carrying out their duties because if you had not managed your five 'ticks' in a specific area listed because, for example, you had been dealing with numerous missing from home enquiries or time had been spent trying to locate a suspect etc, then you were 'underperforming' and thus were given an 'action plan' to make you improve.

The Government and Police now state that they have moved away from 'targets' but, from ex colleagues whom I still know, these 'targets' still exist and are merely 'otherwise described' with new names for them but it's the same old game and they are, from what I have been told as recent as August 2016, just as harsh, if not harsher.

If you still could not satisfy all the ticks in the boxes, despite having genuine and honest reasons for not doing so, you could become subject of 'efficiency regulations' and this was the start of a process where you could effectively be dismissed from the Force when, quite frighteningly, you may have done nothing wrong whatsoever other than carry out your complete Police duties to the full.

This was the start, in my opinion, of a downward destructive slope that would 'chip away' at Officers' confidence and morale over the coming years and lead to a much 'weaker' thin blue line to serve the general public.

I was originally 'head hunted' for the performance role because the then Superintendent knew how good I was at supervising and he had previously been my Inspector on the Alpha Division.

My initial Inspector for this left me to effectively supervise the unit without any incidents and my work was excellent for him, so much so that, when he was not in work for a day or so, I would effectively 'deputise' for him and deal with matters that would normally be of Inspector rank to do so and he was quite confident that these would be competently finalised or progressed by me.

I was extremely welfare orientated not only with my staff that I supervised, but also with any others who chose to confide in me and this did not sit well with bosses because I was again 'treading on toes' of another, perhaps less sympathetic, supervisor but their objections would fall on my 'deaf ears' because, as far as I was concerned, If you supported a member of staff, civilian or Police, then they would remember that and always do their best to give you their utmost capability, something which I still believe in to this date, post Police career.

I had occasion to move an Officer, whom I shall refer to as Constable Summer, who was on 'recuperative duties' due to ill health, from one office and into mine and my rationale was this :-

I had called into the other office to liaise with the Sgt there, Sgt Andrews, and witnessed his hurling sexist comments of many toward the other Officer who just had to 'sit, grin and bear it'.

Well that was not going to happen as far as I was concerned and so I approached her and quietly said "discreetly pack your desk up and bring it to my office where I have four pleasant members of staff and a spare desk which you can use".

This Officer was nearly in tears and immediately carried out my 'order' (it was not an order, it was Mitchell Spence standing up to sexist abuse from someone who was nothing more than an obnoxious bully and, incidentally, was an old 'colleague' of mine from the C.I.D. on the Foxtrot Division, at a time when I had witnessed 'figure manipulation' in relation to T.I.C. offences, need I say more?

So this female Officer carried on her duties in my office free from abuse and appreciated that I had 'stuck my neck on the line' for her, which I did many, many more times for Officers that I came across who were ill or distressed.

I did, however, suffer an attack upon me by two Inspectors as a direct result of my intervention and was threatened with disciplinary proceedings because, in their own words, I had acted 'beyond my authority and role' by carrying out my actions and one, whom I shall refer to as Inspector Friar, stated "you don't know that Officer, she is nothing but trouble and will not move when you ask her to and believe me, you will have to because I am looking into her transfer personally (again off the Division because they see ill Officers as 'liabilities') so you WILL be told to move her and, when she doesn't, I will personally see that you too are dealt with for your arrogance!"

Well, my response was "as far as I am concerned Inspector, you have ignored your duty of care towards that Officer who is suffering from mental illness and it is I that has taken the right and proper course of action and will prove you wrong in time when that time comes".

I was thus 'ordered' to leave their office immediately and I could feel, if feel is the correct terminology to use, his daggers knifing me as I left!

I explained to the Constable what I had just been subjected to and she said "you are the only Sergeant who has taken positive action for me and for that I will never forget! When they do ask me to move office again, I will do so immediately and you will not or should not be subject to any malice because of your empathy and kindness".

When the time came, this Constable did exactly that and, despite my having now been retired for over eighteen months, whenever I see her or chat to her on social networking sites, she still calls me 'Sarge' and says I will 'always be her Sergeant' which I find so very nice, as does my wife because my actions that day made a lasting impression upon her.

Obviously, because of my kindness and empathy towards others, something which has always been in my nature and you could say in my DNA, I was totally in the 'spotlight' of higher ranking Officers whom, I have since learned, referred to me as a 'loose cannon' and a 'time bomb waiting to explode'.

Well, if that is how they wished to describe a decent, honest cop and member of the human race, then so be it because I see this as commendable character traits and nothing will ever change that!

I did learn a grave lesson though as time passed which was that, in the Police, you cannot expect to be treated as you treat others, although this lesson was eventually learnt by my being 'knocked down' many times and getting back up to fight before powers beyond me eventually stopped the 'bout' and I retired on ill health, but that lesson could have cost me my life at my own hands!

Later on in my role, I was to witness my original Performance Unit Inspector become a 'victim' of oppressive bullying by another Superintendent in a performance management meeting who 'belittled' everything that he said purely because he wanted to change the way things were, despite them working fine, because the Superintendent was a 'yes' man and wanted his next rank so change for the sake of change was his way and no doubt ended up on his promotion c.v. (curriculum vitai) too!

I spoke with the Inspector later about how wrong this was and was told "you will get to a point in your career Mitchell when you will just 'sit and take it' because you know if you don't, it will only get worse"

I was extremely shocked and saddened by this because there was a culture now emerging within the Police of 'back stabbers' in bosses who, it seemed, to progress further in their career, would try to 'prove themselves' at other persons' expense, no matter what carnage they left behind and so now the rank structure was 'suspicious' for all concerned, not knowing who to trust or who would 'steal' ideas from others and communication became less prevalent and 'every man (or woman) for themselves' became the hidden motto.

If the leadership at the top of the chain is weak, then this rumbles down through the ranks to the 'foot soldiers' on the ground, the men and women who actually keep our streets safe and the wheels seemed to have been set in motion for this to occur.

This concern I heard on a daily basis from hard working Constables to the effect that they did not know who to trust anymore.

A new Inspector took over in the performance management unit and I shall refer to her as Inspector Sheman.

Not long after taking up her role she even 'queried' the reasons for my depressive illness, which she had no right to do and I found this derogatory and embarrassing as well as challenging my honesty and integrity. I became extremely emotional and broke down and was coolly asked by her if I 'needed some time on my own'.

As a result I spent some considerable time in the then 'GATSO' (traffic camera) office where I suffered a break down and became extremely nervy suffering severe headaches also. Inspector Sheman was not interested in my welfare at all, only her career development.

The following day my health was not good as a direct result of Inspector Sheman the previous day and, although I came into work, I had very cold hands, felt sick and dizzy, my heart was pounding and I was extremely washed out due to lack of sleep overnight caused by the distress of it all.

As a result of this I contacted my then Counsellor and also Occupational Health to arrange appointments to try to cope with this bullying and was told by the paid 'experts' that if the organisation would only leave me alone for a while to recover, then I would stand a fighting chance, but because they insisted on 'attacking' me, any 'foundations' being built for my recovery, were simply being 'blown away'.

As I have said previously, mental illness is not something that you will ever fully recover from and so you learn to live with it and have 'coping mechanisms', but this only works if you are given the 'space' needed for the process and that also involves NOT being queried about the condition from which you suffer unless, and only unless, you divulge this in conversation because, for each day on a recovery that passes, you do feel a little better and as one counsellor told me at a session "if you were flooring your loft, you would do it one plank at a time and one day at a time until, before you know it, you have completed the task and your loft if floored".

That is how any 'recovery' is, day by day and minute by minute and at the very start, you feel so overwhelmed by emotions beyond your control, that you feel totally helpless and vulnerable, but, you will get to a point where you feel able to live a reasonably 'normal' life with the illness, unless, that is, you are a Police Officer as I was because they either did not understand or chose not to!

I subsequently became unfit for work again as a direct result of their arrogance and lack of 'duty of care' which made me feel much worse because the last thing I wanted was to be unfit for duty again.

During my sickness, I had a home visit from Inspector Sheman which she was quite insistent upon carrying out.

Fortunately my federation rep and my wife were also present for this and gave me support because I could not have faced Inspector Sheman on my own at that time!

During this 'home visit', I was told that I would be placed elsewhere due to no places being available on the Lima for me and I was told, quite harshly that it was to be a permanent move and I would not be coming back to that Division.

This was totally done in liaison with Human Resources boss on the Lima, a civilian whom I will refer to as Civvy Baders and Command.

This was totally discriminate to me because other staff had been given positions on Division after illnesses like mine and was a breach of the Disability Discrimination Act (DDA) and also illustrated how the 'organisational representatives' felt that they could break the law passed by Government 'because they could'.

I now hit a new all time low as a direct result of these discriminative attacks upon me and the following morning, when my wife was out at work and the children had gone to school, I shaved all my hair off and cut my head open, then stood in the shower and just let it bleed.

This, I was told at a later time, was a 'self harming' trait that almost everyone who becomes so helpless and distressed will do first.

I was asked if I was going to kill myself by my psychologist whom I will refer to as Dr Dootson which, at the time of doing same, I was seriously considering, but now I felt extremely saddened and humiliated that I could do this and hated the organisational representatives because they were the cause.

My wife broke down in tears when she saw what I had done and could not bring herself to look at me because she was in her own words now 'frightened' of what I may do to myself next'!

I needed help, understanding and support from Division and the Organisation and all I was getting was abuse and neglect.

On 12th July, 2005 after returning to work, which in itself was traumatic after being off, I had a meeting with a Chief Inspector whom I shall refer to as Ch. Insp. Patricks and he agreed that I would be able to be in civilian clothes rather than uniform whilst I settled back in for as long as I needed and that I would be in the Operational Policing Unit (OPU) doing supervision of the stop and account forms.

I was to have another meeting with him and Human Resources manager civvy Baders the following day.

The above meeting went ahead and I was informed by both civvy Baders and Chief Inspector Patricks that it was not a permanent role, merely a temporary placing and not for a Sgt.

This was in contradiction of what I had been told by Chief Inspector Patricks the previous day that I was a Lima Division Officer and would be looked after on my return to work.

Civvy Baders told me that they had put together an action plan for me to sign which continued a review of my role and hours in 28 days.

I was informed by them that my hours would be increased to 6 and then 8 and I told both of them that this was against the medical advice of the Force Psychiatrist, whom I shall refer to as Dr Strikeman and against the Force Medical Officer Dr Slades instructions that were forwarded on official medical advice forms to civvy Baders in Human Resources.

This stated that I should start at 4 hours to the next medical review which would have been in 6 to 8 weeks from the date of same, thus my next review would have been the October. Civvy Baders stated that this would not be soon enough and I tried to explain that if they put pressure on me like that, it would affect my psychological state of mind and that this is why I had been told on professional medical advice by both Dr Strikeman and Dr Slade that this was extremely important and I should be kept in a local area in surroundings that I was familiar with and also familiar people.

I told civvy Baders and Chief Inspector Patricks that I was feeling insecure by their suggestions and knew that my mind would start racing making me feel ill again and that I was not trying to obstruct my return to work, and that I had no physical injuries and it was my mind and well being that they were interfering with.

Civvy Baders quite firmly stated that the Drs form showed 4 hours and I had to correct her for my own sanity and well being informing her that it stated NO MORE THAN 4 HOURS and that it gave me the opportunity if I had a bad day, to remove myself from the work place.

I was then told by them to allow a short while for them both to discuss this without my being present.

As a result of the above, I went and rang Occupational Health and asked them to ring me back on my mobile phone after explaining what was happening. I spoke with the OHU and they confirmed my thoughts of same.

I also tried to make an earlier appointment to see Dr Slade regarding this matter because I was worried, but no earlier appointments could be made and the OHU also stated that civvy Baders should e- mail the OHU with Divisions intentions PRIOR to implementing same so that medical advice could be sought.

This they were not doing because, as far as they were concerned, they wanted to put enough pressure onto me so that I would 'break' and then they could place me onto either disciplinary regulations or efficiency regulations, either way I could lose my job, you see, this is how my Police Force, certainly the Lima Division, dealt with people who suffered mental illness and were 'liabilities' to 'the organisation' or 'loose cannons' as they referred to me!

When I returned to civvy Baders and Chief Inspector Patricks, I informed them of the OHU directions and civvy Baders demanded "Why have you done that?"
I explained that this was because, yet again, they had made me feel as though I was being awkward and so I needed to clarify this.
Civvy Baders queried why she had to e mail occupational health regarding her intentions and became very awkward because her decision was being questioned.

I was then informed that the 28 day review had been reasonable as had the increase in hours but that I would now have to be reviewed week commencing August, 2005.

They then gave me a letter to sign and a copy which I refused to do because it had a paragraph stating that my role was temporary and was not a Sgt post and that if Division could not find a place for me, it would have to be looked into at Force Level and if there was nothing available, then I WOULD HAVE TO GO SICK!

This I found to be pressurising me into going sick, which I did not want to do because I was trying to return to work not stay off and as I have stated in previous chapters, I always believed in 'a good days work for a good days pay', nothing more and most certainly nothing less.

I took the letter but with no intention of agreeing to this plan of intended actions and I felt that this was a step towards 'efficiency regulations' (Capability Proceedings) and evidence to me that Division were looking at me as a Liability not an Investment, yet, quite hypocritically, my Police Force had been previously awarded an 'Investors In People' charter mark.

The pressure was continued to be applied to me by H.R. civvy Baders and I was summonsed to see her by the assistant H.R. manager and was faced with "Come in and close the door and take a seat".

This meeting turned out to be a 'review of my role in the OPU which should have been done by the Inspector whom I shall refer to as Inspector Norbert, but he was 'engaged', well that is the story that I was told anyway.

This review was not supposed to be until a much later date and during this I was then told by civvy Baders that there was 'no role on the lima division' for me and now she was going to look force wide for me which caused me distress because of my previous incident with Inspector Sheman, when Human Resources, (civvy Baders) had said exactly the same then!

Civvy Baders completed a form to send to the Attendance Management Unit team, (AMU) which was again in <u>total contradiction</u> to the professional medical advice given by both Dr Strikeman and Dr Slade and their next medical review was only due in OCTOBER 2005!
They had now begun the process of 'closing ranks' on me and, in my opinion, believed that they were a 'law unto themselves'.

I was also told that my 'performance' was not 'up to expectations' of someone with a mental disorder and that, I felt, was extremely insulting not only to myself, but to all other people who suffered in this way and had the same 'stigma' attached as I was now experiencing!

'I WAS NOT UP TO EXPECTATIONS OF SOMEONE WITH A MENTAL DISORDER'! Can you believe it?

A pattern of 'extermination' was now emerging against me and most importantly, my mental health, but this was not the worst to come, by no means, however, at that particular time in my life, I was not to know this.

Within most Organisations, there are systems or procedures in place to help employees 'have a voice' should something occur that they are not comfy with and in my Force, there was a 'Grievance Procedure' for such and so on in September, 2005, I duly undertook this and submitted an in depth report about the way in which I was being treated, hoping that some 'middle ground' may be reached, but I should have known better than to hope for that really because this was not to be.

The following day, I saw my then Superintendent whom I shall refer to as Supt. Halton regarding my Grievance and he was very apologetic

and agreed with me that it seemed that 'heads had got together' before he had seen the report and the answers/excuses given by H.R and others were viable.
Supt. Halton also stated to me that the individuals concerned had been 'very clever' in how they had done what they had done resulting in there being little he could do to assist me.

I felt disgusted by this because 'confidentiality' was now an issue for me, although I was quite happy that Supt. Halton did not do anything malicious in the 'Grievance' process and had been Independent and professional.

Later in his career, he too, was attacked by the 'Organisation' and moved from the Lima to an inner city area for 'developmental' purposes which was, in my opinion, most definitely a conspiracy against him because it was fact that he was due to retire within 12 - 18 months and had told me that he had no inclination to progress to the next rank of Chief Superintendent whatsoever.

I have to give him my full respect because, during a retirement speech by another, Superintendent Halton spoke aloud and made sure his disgust about his 'developmental' move was known to all present, but that is how he was, what you saw, you got and he was not the type of person to 'stab you in the back' or take a 'beating' from higher ranks without going down with a fight!

This was what the 'organisation' and its representatives were now trying to bring through the Police, a 'generation' of 'yes' men and women for want of a better way to describe them, who were no more than 'puppets' having their strings operated by either high ranking Officers or representatives of Constitutional Policy makers and that is most certainly not the way to allow a Police Force (I'm sick of referring to it as a 'service'!) to operate because the only people that will suffer in the long term will be those who stand up to be counted, as I did, and, more importantly, the PUBLIC because the service they receive will diminish and the streets they knew as once 'safe' would now become 'dangerous' for them and their families.
The Police Federation of England and Wales stated in 2014 that one city, Manchester, was now a 'no go' area after midnight because they just did not have enough Officers to Police it safely anymore!

Violent crime reducing with Burglaries and other 'monitored' crimes? That I will cover in some depth in a later chapter of this book when I was National Crime Recording Standards Sergeant because I fought some very, very harsh 'battles' whilst on the Lima Division against figure manipulation and reclassification of crimes reported so that they were categorised as less serious, but I stood my ground and that was one of the 'final nails to put in my occupational coffin' really, but read that later because I am certain that it will astonish you considerably.

Anyway, back to my then Superintendent Halton.

His mistake, if you read it as a mistake, was to stand up against the organisation and in particular, as he told anyone who had asked, which I did, an Assistant Chief Constable of my Force, when they were on a visit to the Lima Division and he spoke against what they were 'preaching' as the way forward, despite that being the worst way possible to go and so, as far as I was concerned, he had done exactly what I did regularly, which was not to 'sing the organisational song' or 'go with the flow' when you knew it was wrong, corrupt or immoral and it seemed that the Organisation and its 'nodding dog' representatives within the higher ranks, despised this and the individuals concerned to the core and would then go all out to destroy their career or make life as difficult as possible for them.

The attack upon me continued and I was placed onto 'efficiency regulations' stage 1, the first of 3 or 4 steps to 'remove' an individual from the Police Force, but I still fought on and this is where I utilised the services of the Police Federation, something which I am extremely grateful because, without their assistance, advice and subsequently excellent legal services, I would either have committed suicide or been Imprisoned for a criminal allegation which was untrue, but that will be enhanced upon later in the book with references to another Constable referred to as 'B.B', (Bunny Boiler) and believe me, that Officer was extremely dangerous and, I suspected, corrupt and passing on information to others whom I suspected were in the criminal fraternity!

I had also now begun recording any conversations that I had with bosses or H.R. managers to protect myself because, when you use a voice activated recorder and place it in front of a boss, they suddenly go 'on the back foot' and do, most times, treat you somewhat more 'gently' because they know that what they say could come back and 'bite them on the ass'!

This I carried with me at all times because, in my mind, this was my shield from the abuse and oppression I was now being subjected to!

Chief Insp.Patricks had now decided that, until he could 'fathom out' what to do with me, I should go home on 'garden leave', something which was never heard of in the Police, but at least it meant that I was out of the 'spotlight' for a little while and at that moment in time, that suited me fine because I had been, unbeknown to the oppressors, very 'close to the edge' and, if they had just pressured me a little more, all be it wrong, then I might just have broken down, but, gladly, they never knew just how close they had come to their aim to destroy my mental health!

On 18/10/09 I received a phone call whilst on 'garden leave' from Ch. Insp. Patricks asking to come and see me.

I refused his 'request' because he wanted to talk about the previous days' meeting and I was extremely nervous and told him I was shaking, had cold hands and a dry mouth just by talking to him.

I had lost trust in the Organisation because of how I had been dealt with and was frightened by this.
Ch. Insp. Patricks therefore told me that Command and Human Resource (Civillian Baders), had made the decision that I should be on sick leave and not 'garden leave' and so as of this date, that is exactly what would occur!

I refused this stating that I was not sick and had been sent home as a result of a direct order until I saw Dr Strikeman the following Friday. Ch. Insp. Patrick' stated that a letter would be dropped off at my house and this letter contained many discrepancies concerning my circumstances.

The letter made me look as if I was not helping myself so they could presumably get me to stage 3 of the efficiency regulations and thus I would have to either resign or be dismissed!
I felt totally betrayed by the organisation and that pressure was deliberately being applied to me by Human Resources (civilian Baders) and Ch. Insp. Patricks.

I subsequently wrote in my pocket note book "I DO NOT DESERVE THIS TREATMENT".

On 19/10/05, after seeking advice from the Police Federation (fed), I went into work to do a 10am - 3pm shift because I was not sick and was most definitely NOT having bosses thinking that they could 'force' me onto sick leave!

I was immediately informed by another Sgt that the operations Ch. Insp. whom I shall refer to as Ch. Insp. Smallman wished to see me and so, despite my suspecting what was to face me, I went to see him and saw that he had the Detective Ch. Insp. whom I shall refer to as D.C.I. Kurt present.

I was asked why I was in and I told them I was there to work!

Forcibly and strongly I was told by one of them that I had been 'ordered' to go home by Ch. Insp. Patricks and had not followed that 'order'.

This was now becoming somewhat oppressive towards me and so I made an excuse to go and get the letter above but instead, I got my voice recorder and returned to the 'fire' so to speak!

I placed the recorder on the desk and switched it on in front of me, telling both of the bosses that I was recording this for my accuracy and assistance because I was unconfident.

I also stated that the Federation had advised that they would speak to them if needed, but neither would do so and I was immediately and firmly again told I was to GO HOME!
This frightened and unnerved me extremely and so I used my mobile to ring the Federation as well as recording all on my voice recorder and relayed to them what I was being faced with.
The Federation heard the tone of the conversation and asked me to query if I was to go home on sick or just go home.

It was established that I was now advised to go home and NOT SICK or annual leave, just to go home and await further contact from a senior ranking Officer after I had seen the Force Psychiatrist Dr Strikeman, as arranged.

The Federation advised me to do this and just before I did, I was told by Ch. Insp. 'J.K' that I "WOULD BE ESCORTED OFF THE PREMISES" by DCI Kurt which made me feel totally undermined and attacked and as if I had been suspended, having only been in work for less than 1 hour!

When I went to get changed out of my uniform DCI Kurt came to see me in the locker room and said "THIS IS NOT A PERSONAL ATTACK ON YOU", however, the way I was made to feel as degraded and almost a criminal, my confidence was again damaged further and it certainly felt personal!

Whilst I was being 'escorted' from the Police station, I was seen by a good colleague of mine who was the Field Intelligence Officer (F.I.O) and another Constable.
I felt totally humiliated by the whole bullying and harassing experience, yet I was nothing to the bosses who were treating me like this!

I wrote in my pocket book "I NEED HELP, NOT THREATS, WHY DON'T THEY LISTEN?"

Because Division and Human Resources (civilian Baders) had not done anything to arrange a case conference (recommended by the Force Medical Officers and also something that would illustrate any 'duty of care' towards me by the 'Organisation'), I faxed Occupational Health and demanded one because I felt that this was now the only way I could make the Organisation and Division realise that I was ill.

It was as though Division did not want to participate in any process other than my 'removal' and this was a perfect example of how mental health was dealt with by them!

I wrote in my pocket note book, "I DO NOT WANT TO DO ANY HARM TO MYSELF BUT AM CONSTANTLY SEEING NO WAY OUT OF THIS VICIOUS CIRCLE BECAUSE THEY JUST WONT LISTEN TO ME -- WHY NOT?"

This was how their campaign of abuse and oppression was affecting my state of mind and my family was seeing a very different person to the loving husband and father that my wife and children knew, in fact, my wife, who had by now on several occasions broken down in tears, regularly said "it's like the lights are on but no one is at home when I look at you!"

In October I received 2 letters in the post, one telling me that I was on half pay as of 01/11/05 and another from Roll call(resource management) asking for a sick note!

By this time I was taking prescribed medication of 150mg Venlafaxine Anti Depressants and 5mg Diazepam, ALL AS A RESULT OF THE ORGANISATIONS' TREATMENT OF ME!!

I was not sick and so contacted the Federation (fed) for advice and help due to being oppressed into submission by the Organisation and not recovering fast enough for them!

I wrote in my pocket note book "IS THAT MY FAULT, THEY MADE ME FEEL IT IS BY NOT UNDERSTANDING MY POINTS AND CONCERNS".

I also wrote "TO THIS DATE 28/10/05 I HAVE 20 YEARS LOYAL SERVICE IN: - THIS IS HOW THEY THANK YOU!"

I rang the Force Human Resources Department and explained as best I could that what was happening to me COULD NOT BE RIGHT.

The representative for Force H.R. went to liaise with her colleagues and came back with the answer that DIVISION ARE WRONG AND THEY SHOULD HAVE PUT ME ON RESTRICTED DUTIES UNTIL I SAW THE FORCE MEDICAL OFFICER, DR 'Z' AND THAT THEY COULD NOT PUT SOMEONE ONTO SICK LEAVE AGAINST THEIR WILL!!

I informed the Fed rep and he subsequently e mailed civilian Baders regarding the unlawful actions that they were doing and there was no regulation allowing this!

I was now having serious Domestic problems because of the pressure placed upon me by my Force and was deteriorating in my mental health, but they just did not care and as far as they were concerned, they could do WHATEVER THEY LIKED to me and any other Officers who 'opposed' their ways!

At the beginning of November, the welfare section of the O.H.U. Contacted me to inform me a case conference had finally been arranged with extensive reluctance and resistance and was to be held on 04/11/05.

I had a battle with Ch. Insp. Patricks and H. R. (civilian Baders) to get persons relevant to me to be able to attend because they just wanted the 'Organisations' representatives present, but I insisted on my psychologist, psychiatrist, force Dr, welfare rep, Fed rep and most importantly, my wife to be present, and Civilian Baders and Ch. Insp. Patricks certainly were not happy about this whatsoever!

There was no way that I was going to attend a case conference concerning my situation and future unless all experts were present to counter any comments made by the 'Organisational representatives' and had refused to attend unless this occurred, well, after all, they would not have been able to continue without the 'subject' being there now would they?

Christmas was soon approaching and one of my children wanted a pair of 'gothic' boots for this which cost then, approximately fifty pounds, but because they had overheard me talking with my wife about my imminent fall onto half pay, they came to us, tears welling in their eyes and said they now did not want them because it would waste our money that was precious to us.

They were only 13 at the time!

Upon hearing this, my eyes welled up with tears because this was now causing me more psychological torture hearing my child and possibly my other child when they became aware, not wanting Christmas presents' because they knew what was happening to me!

I went into the bathroom to avoid them noticing my upset and immediately broke down in tears....all down to bad management not wishing to comply with the legislation and procedures laid down for exactly my situation and that of others!

The case conference went ahead on 04/11/05 and the resultant consequences for this bad management was Ch. Insp. Patricks had to apologise on record, for the way he, civilian Baders and Division had handled my situation and this was brought about by the experts present warning of the damage they (management) were causing my psychological and physical health.

In Ch. Insp. Patricks own words he said "IN MITCHELLS CASE, WE GOT IT WRONG!" and apologised for this error in their judgement, which was like 'closing the stable door when the horse had bolted' because the damage they had done to my family and I so far would take many, many years to repair!

The Police Federation challenged my sickness and half pay issues and the Force / Division were given a choice of either reimbursing my wages, amending my sickness record to remove the applicable days OR FACE COURT ACTION after reminding them of a recent West Midlands case similar to mine that was just recently settled out of court on the day of proceedings!

It seems to always be the case that people in 'power' will refuse to back down despite their being wrong, until they have absolutely nowhere else to go and it took a legal notice from the Federation solicitors, to do exactly that!

So Division and civilian Baders chose to back down and resolve the matter without court, but they will push all the way even when they don't know what they are doing because how dare anyone 'challenge' them!

Well, despite my health suffering, I DARED and so these were two 'battles' won for me in a way, but there were many, many more to come!

I was also conscious of the fact that, if I stood up against them, then perhaps it would make them change their ways concerning how others in the future were treated, well that was my hope anyway.

When someone is wrong in the way they deal with an individual, or worse still, malicious and deceitful in their ways, and have been 'highlighted' as such, you would think that they would accept 'defeat', but no, civilian Baders had other ideas for me and I had several more 'minor scuffles' with her and the 'Organisation' before they seemed to leave me alone, alone that is, until a Constable whom I suspected was corrupt, (B.B.) attempted to destroy my career and family and sank to very dark depths to do so, which will be expanded upon later in the following chapters.

On 02/11/05 the Federation sent me civilian Baders response to their info that management could not put anyone on sick leave.

The response was that "IN HER OPINION, I SHOULD BE ON SICK LEAVE AND FOLLOW FORCE PROCEDURES FOR SUCH".

Civilian Baders just would not step down from her stance and she had total disregard to regulations that were there to protect Officers as well as assist the organisation.
Can you believe it, a civilian in a high position attempting to 'make her own laws and procedures', rather than complying with legislation and policy!

Many, many years ago Police Officers were replaced with civilians for certain roles such as Local Intelligence Office (L.I.O.) and filing etc, so when the 'old coppers' who had done those, retired, the civilian would step into their shoes and this meant not having to take another Police Officer from operational duties to do that.

This, in itself, was a good thing, however, the balance became so very, very wrong and it was heading towards more civilian employees than Police Officers at some stations and as well as this, vast skills were being lost, all in the name of 'cost cutting'!

I recall many a 'battle' with the Lima Administration Officer, a civilian, who would fight 'tooth and nail' to avoid you obtaining enough uniform to do your job and it was almost like the money was coming out of his own pockets, yet he would think nothing of purchasing something new regularly for his 'civvy staff' presumably at the expense of Police Officers uniforms because it all came out of the 'Divisional budget'!

We, the Police Officers, had had enough of this and soon came around to devising our own 'requisition' system for much needed uniforms and it was simple really, ring the Administration Manager (civilian), obtain your authority for the small amount of items that he had reluctantly approved, wait for your signed requisition form to be sent to you, and then add all the uniform you really needed because, by the time it was returned to the Divisional Admin Manager (D.A.M), it was too late, you had all your required uniform to effectively carry out your duties and well, if he complained or ranted at you, you just smiled and walked away!

There was nothing illegal in this, it was not deception or fraud as it is referred to now, because it was all property of the Force and, well, you wouldn't go out on a Saturday night to a night club wearing a 'job' shirt or trousers now, would you so, as you can see, it could not be abused illegally!

CHAPTER TWELVE – THE CRIME EVALUATORS AND NATIONAL CRIME RECORDING SERGEANT (N.C.R.S)

After some considerable psychological help from qualified experts, I seemed to be on the 'road to recovery' and was getting my life and career back on track and was offered the position of National Crime Recording Standard Sgt after being 'head hunted' by new DCI whom I shall refer to as DCI Whistler and was given responsibility of training all staff in NCRS and improving the Divisions Performance in this area.

The DCI knew me when I was in the Custody Office and, at that time he was also a Sgt and was aware of how hard I worked, as did the new Ch. Supt. who had also been a Sgt and so for the immediate future I was again left alone by Command to carry out my work.

Both these 'bosses' were on the 'fast track' promotion scheme but they were both ordinary Officers who had not lost sight of their roots and were good to work with!

Although I was based in the Crime Evaluators Unit which consisted of six Constables, I was not at that time responsible for them and, with hindsight, wished I never had been.

I spent my initial months researching what N.C.R.S. was all about and attended the Force crime registrars' office responsible for overseeing the whole Force and the way in which the various divisions recorded crimes.

N.C.R.S. was a Government initiated process which focussed upon the 'victim' of a crime' (in theory) and thus, if a victim reported a crime, then, unless there was evidence to show otherwise, that crime would be recorded and, wherever possible, investigated, which was much better than the account earlier in this book about how rape victims, for example, were treated and so now I felt that, despite only being a Sergeant in rank, I could make that difference that I had always set my mind upon doing because my role was an extremely important and influential one which gave me the power, in theory, to be able to 'overturn' decisions regarding victims and crimes recorded for the better!

This was to become my 'forte' and, no matter what I came up against, I would ensure that the past corrupt ways of recording and detecting crimes would be completely destroyed.

The role was linked to the crime evaluators because it was they who would decide whether or not to return a crime to an Officer for further investigation or to file it as 'undetected' and this, they had been allowed to do for many years, unsupervised directly, which was not the best way because Officers each knew who their 'favourite' evaluator was and who they could 'sweet talk' into their way of thinking and vice-versa!

This meant that 'old school' cops would be able to try to 'write off' crimes perhaps because they felt that it was not worth their time investigating them and, on the other hand, evaluators could 'hide- away' crimes that they had similar thoughts about which was not how things should be done because EVERY victim is as important as the other and must be treated as such and so, as my role became more 'real' so did my influence and I suggested that I should be directly responsible for all the crime evaluators and that they should, in return, be accountable to me for their decision making!
I would carry out 'dip samples' of crimes recorded and evaluated to ensure that the correct actions were being taken, but this was seen by some evaluators as 'spying' on them, which was not the case after all, if you are doing your job as it should be, then there is no reason for you to be worried, unless, of course, you weren't and that is what I was finding where one Officer whom I refer to as Constable B.B. was concerned.

This idea was embraced quite willingly by DCI Whistler with the understanding that if ever I felt this was becoming a strain upon my mental health, then I was to let him know immediately because he was fully aware of the trauma that I had experienced and became somewhat of a 'guardian' for me which prevented civvy '1' and others in their hateful vengeance towards me and, in return for his 'protection', I vowed that I would give him exactly what he expected from me and more, to go the 'extra mile' as it were.

So, the news was delivered to the evaluators and let's just say they regarded this as a 'slap in the face', but, in my opinion, it was a necessity to ensure that the public (victims of crime) were given the service that they deserved, which was in dire need of improvement at that time!

The evaluators consisted of four policewomen (two of which were 'old school' and did not like change),one who was suffering from 'alcoholism' which in itself is an illness and one who was relatively young in service but allegedly could not patrol on the streets because of injuries to her knees (yet that individual was able to attend a gymnasium and, wearing knee straps that sports personalities use, exercised quite freely on machines that utilised exactly the same ligaments and muscles as you would do when patrolling on the streets) and on 'social nights out' would find it no problem whatsoever to dance for considerable amounts of time, but she had, in my opinion, played the 'disability card' against the 'Organisation' and regularly made it known that if anyone ever challenged her, then she would, in her own words, "take them to an industrial tribunal"!

Now I am totally supportive of people who have genuine disabilities, but I had witnessed, first hand, that Officer 'working out' at the gym because I had joined it too as a way of maintaining my mental health well being and I strongly believe that this individual felt 'threatened' by me which will account for my treatment at the hands of the 'Organisation' later in this book when the same Officer made a serious and totally false set of criminal allegations against me and the history preceding that action will most certainly open your eyes, I strongly believe, into how good the Police Organisation are in 'closing of ranks' when dealing with 'employees' whom they see as a 'threat' to the way they work!

The remaining staff consisted of two male Officers, one of whom was severely disabled physically after being subjected to hospital procedures that had gone wrong and a young civilian and I embraced them all with 'open arms' and told them that, whilst I was there to be in direct supervision of them, I was not someone who made change for change sake and unless I observed something that was in need of improving, then they would be able to continue in their work as if I was not present and I believed that this would 'placate' them, but that was not the case and it took me quite some time to gain their 'trust'.

Don't get me wrong, I had seen areas that were in need of change and work practises also that had to cease, but I was not going to go in all heavy handed because I wanted these staff members to work with me and not against me!

There is a saying 'keep your friends close and your enemies even closer' and, as time progressed, that was to be shown as extremely accurate.

Whilst in my role, I had to deal with many, many welfare issues namely childcare 'issues' with Constable B.B. although as time progressed, I found that almost everything became an issue for this Officer and they 'needed' to be the centre of attention and on the receiving end of colleagues sympathies to feel 'complete', so much so that on one occasion where this Officer was 'overtly' upset, even her husband said to me " everything is fine, but you know what (B.B.) is like!"

Whilst working with the Evaluation staff, we all bought each other presents on birthdays and the like and this seemed to keep a viable working relationship alive, however, on my birthday, Constable B.B. bought me, separately from the others, a bottle of 'D.K.N.Y' 'Delicious' eau de toilette, which I thought was a little excessive and then kept making comments about how 'delicious' I smelt, something which unsettled me somewhat, but I tried to 'laugh it off'.

I became very uncomfortable when this Officer told me that she wore the 'female version' of the 'D.K.N.Y' and that they should always be put 'together', but I believed that I could 'distance' myself from such comments with laughter and jokes!
I came to learn, by serious error of professional judgement that Constable B.B. seemed to have, in fact, narcissistic characteristics, which became extremely severe towards me as you will see later in the chapters of this book!

If you research narcissist on the internet, you will see that they always want to be 'centre of attention', 'latch on' to people whether the individual likes that or not and, should you upset someone with such tendencies, then they will become extremely hostile and even dangerous toward you!

There were issues of domestic abuse and alcoholism with one Constable, bullying and harassment with the young civilian to illustrate just a few, so you can perhaps understand how complex and 'testing' times these were, but, you carry on and strive to deliver the best service that you possibly can to both your colleagues and the members of public who, as far as I was concerned, were of the utmost importance!
I would treat everyone whom I dealt with as equal and favour nobody and this was true both on duty and off.
There was an occasion where a meeting was to be held concerning the 'working procedures' of the crime evaluators and I was approached by one Constable who stated that she was representing all the evaluators by suggesting, without directly saying it, that the meeting should take place without Constable B.B present and, because I was a fair supervisor, I addressed each and every member of staff under my supervision and made them all totally clear that I would not accept 'exclusions' such as was being suggested ever occurring, but, looking back, I can see why that had been requested however hindsight is a wonderful thing isn't it?

Every other year, my wife and I held a 'summer party' at our home (a garden party really) and invited friends, neighbours, family and work colleagues and on two occasions, Constable B.B. came with her husband and, without any inaccuracy here, everybody who met her, took a dislike to her because of the way she wanted to be centre of attention and would 'interrupt' conversations just to become 'involved'.
We have a 'hot tub' which we allowed people to use if they brought the appropriate swimwear and, whilst two good male friends were in this playing cards, Constable B.B. climbed in almost fully de-clothed, much to the shock of our good friends and, well I do not really wish to enhance on the way she was, but suffice to say, her husband was extremely embarrassed about it and had to 'drag' her out, dress her and take her to an awaiting taxi!

My wife had even been approached by Constable B.B. on numerous occasions at out parties, saying how she wished that she had a daughter like us because she only had sons, how lucky my wife was to have me as her husband and how kind and considerate I was which, B.B. said, was totally different to her husband whom she was even suggesting might be interested in men rather than herself and this worried her!

With hindsight, I should have heeded my wife and our friends' 'warnings' about this individual, but I believed in treating everyone equally and put her actions and demeanour down to 'too much alcohol', which was most definitely a wrong decision made by me as further in you will understand.

I brought the young civilian from the C.I.D. office and into one nearer to the evaluators because he was being subjected to offensive harassment (which seemed to be the 'norm' where 'old school' Officers were concerned especially with C.I.D past and present and it was affecting his work, yet he would not ask for help, but I just knew that if someone did not act, things could become very sinister indeed.
The latest harassment to have occurred was that his 'warrant card' had been defaced and a note had been attached to it saying "also an excuse for an employee" or similar!

Well, I would not tolerate this type of malice and, although some may say it is just 'innocent banter', I would have to disagree because, when things get personal, as they seemed to be doing here with this civilian, then it is only a matter of time before it affects not only your work, but your home and, most importantly, your family and I was not prepared to allow this, having been subjected to such like in my career and now being in a position where I could do something positive to stop it!

I seized the warrant card and note and placed it in an evidence bag with a secure tag so that it could be fingerprinted to identify the culprit or culprits and deal effectively with them for their unprofessionalism.
In good faith I then informed my Detective Inspector, referred to as D.I. 'M.N' and, well would you have guessed it, I was asked not to pursue the matter any further and it would be dealt with by him and the Detective Sergeant (whom I believe now, had had a hand in the issue).

After a few days, the D.I. reported back that nobody had owned up to the 'misdemeanour' (no surprise there really) and that the Detective Sergeant (D.S.) had 'advised' all staff not to be 'childish'!
I do not really think childish describes the actions effectively really, especially when act like this can progress and those affected by it can succumb to 'self harming' thoughts!

When I explained this to the civilian, he had already been 'spoken to' by the D.S. and D.I. so it's no surprise really that he said he accepted it was 'just good fun'!

In 2007, Constable B.B, whom I was now supervising and was pregnant, rang the office on her way into work to explain that 'her waters had broken' but that she was still going to come in and 'see how things go' which I thought rather unusual because, being a father myself, I remember that when waters go on a pregnant woman, then it is usually the start of the labour process and normally people make their way into hospital, but not Constable B.B.

It was only at a later date, when other things were emerging, that I realised she was yet again 'playing the system' and, having come into work, knew that this would not be classed as a 'maternity day' because she was in work and then had had to leave, but, when you read later how deceitful and dishonest this Officer could be, this will come as no surprise to you!

Anyway, I did what any decent person and, whilst the Officer was travelling into work, rang the hospital, explained who I was and the circumstances unfolding and ensured that there would be medical staff available to assist her once she attended.
This course of action, and the next, I would do for any female member of staff who had obviously gone into labour because that is the type of person that those who know me well, will tell you I am.
As soon as Constable B.B. came into work, I immediately turned her around and took her in my car and to hospital (I did not believe an ambulance would attend and did not want any further risks being taken so chose to drive).
Constable B.B. was kept in and I then made enquiries to locate her husband, also a serving Officer, who was on a training day, so that he could get to her soonest!
Roughly four hours later, they had a baby son and I was asked to be the Godfather!

To this date, I wish I had not accepted that request, but I felt slightly 'honoured' that they had asked me because of the actions I had taken and also slightly 'obliged' and they were 'putting' upon my general good nature saying "if you had not done what you had, then it might be a different scenario and we are so grateful to you", well, that was what Constable B.B. told me on both their behalf, but, as I was to learn much later on, there was an 'ulterior' motive to her actions and, for the only time ever, I was stupid enough to ignore advice and also my 'gut feeling', which I will never do again!

Whilst carrying out my role as N.C.R.S. Sgt, I would sift through the incidents that Officers had attended during the previous 24 hours or since my last tour of duty (T.O.D.) and ensure that they had dealt with them correctly and that the necessary crimes reported by victims had been recorded.

If I came across any incidents that I felt should have had a crime report recorded, but it had not been, then I would personally contact the victim and ascertain what had occurred.
If I was satisfied that the matter had been dealt with correctly, then I would endorse the incident log accordingly, but, if I was not satisfied, then I would contact the Officer concerned together with their immediate supervisor to ask questions and, in the majority of cases, a crime or crimes would be submitted and the matter would be closed to my satisfaction.

There were times though when I came into conflict, especially where C.I.D. were involved, because they did not wish a crime to be recorded or were 'delaying' its submission until they or their bosses (D.I. or D.C.I.) were satisfied that one should go in!

Well this was not how N.C.R.S. was supposed to work because, if a victim reported a crime, then it must be submitted unless the Officer in the case found information or evidence to the contrary and then the incident log would be endorsed with such information to negate any crime submission.

I would still 'review' that incident and only endorse it if it was correct and I had the Force Crime Registrars authority to do so!

C.I.D. however, wanted to 'tweak' that ruling to suit their end 'goal' which was to reduce crime and so they would 'advise' Officers NOT to submit certain crimes until they had 'looked into things' and this usually would take longer than the time period allowed, which was 72 hours, from a victim reporting a crime until its submission and so, you can probably see, this was to throw me into much conflict, from which, by doing my job as it was supposed to be done, I made more 'enemies within'!

Local 'policies and procedures' were also introduced by C.I.D. bosses such as certain crimes must have the D.I. involved for advice prior to submission and, in an attempt to reduce theft from the person crimes, an Officer was allocated to 'revisit' all the victims who reported theft of mobile phones in an 'attempt' to persuade them that 'perhaps' the mobiles had been lost and then the crimes could be 'written off' as 'no crime'!
I had to speak to many an upset victim of these types of crime because of this, in my opinion 'dubious' policy.

That was a totally unacceptable to me and, in my opinion, corrupt, because the original Officer in the case had, from my own reviews of some of these crimes that they were trying to 'write off', carried out diligent enquiries and was satisfied, as I was, that the phones in question had been stolen and not 'lost'.

How low would 'Organisational representatives' go to reduce their crimes recorded?

Even most recently (January 24th, 2013) the Media has reported that the Office of National Statistics suspect that the crimes recorded by the Police are not necessarily an accurate figure to illustrate that crime has reduced because they have compared this to a survey carried out with members of the public which asked 'have you been a victim of crime' and the response clearly suggested possible 'ambiguities' in the Police figures and that of the public feedback and, in my opinion, the practises I challenged within my own Force, as is usually the case from historic illustrations, are possibly occurring on a National scale because when one Police Force 'reduce' their crime figures, others in a similar 'family group' (a cluster of Forces with the same or similar issues/problems/trends etc), will copy what they see as 'best practise because, after all, it has brought results to the originating Force, whether morally right or wrong!

This was to be 'fuel to the fire' for H.R. and those others in positions higher than mine, at a later time, in their attempts to destroy my career, my family and, most importantly, myself.

Things were progressing satisfactory and I felt that I was coping well, until changes occurred in the command and my immediate supervisors which then allowed certain crime evaluators to 'take advantage' of this.

I now had an 'acting' D.C.I. (a D.I. who is temporarily carrying out the role of the next rank to assist in their own promotion), whom I shall refer to as acting D.C.I. Lewis and a newly promoted female D.I and things began to get intimidating!

Three female evaluators, of which Constable B.B. was one, would 'favour' going to see the new D.I. regarding matters rather than me which was totally incorrect procedures to follow and showed me to have a 'lack of supervisory skills' in the words of the female D.I. and so I made strong representations that she should be directing these staff back to me and 'supporting' my role and rank, rather than was the case now, giving the advice and then criticising me.

Constable B.B. would 'flirt' with the 'acting' D.C.I. Lewis and talk to him about his like of horses, which on its own would seem innocent enough, BUT, she would then, as I heard with my own ears most uncomfortably when he was in the evaluators office to talk about a crime, bring in suggestions of how good he must look in his riding gear, especially with 'the whip' and she emphasised 'the whip' very strongly and gave him a 'smirk' which, in my own opinion, was a direct reference to sexual preferences!

I did challenge Acting D.C.I. Lewis regarding this at a later date, but he denied, as Constable B.B. did, the conversation ever occurring.

From enquiries made, of which I made a formal complaint through the I.P.C.C. (Independent Police Complaints Commission), Constable B.B. had previously 'had a relationship with a previous D.C.I. which was very common knowledge amongst C.I.D. staff and several evaluators as well as Federation Reps and had been 'protected' by same whilst seconded in (placed temporarily) to serious crime investigations as a typist or clerk because of her 'restricted duties' due to debilitating knee injuries and so, I believed, that perhaps she was attempting this with the acting D.C.I. who began to take more of an interest in her wellbeing more so than other staff, male or female!

Whilst carrying out my duties, I observed Constable B.B. on the Police computer accessing information, which, in the normal course of her duties, is acceptable, but, on numerous occasions, she was talking about crimes on her mobile phone and these calls always seemed to be in full flow as I returned into the office after having been engaged elsewhere and when no other staff were present.
As soon as I returned, Constable B.B. would 'terminate' her call rather abruptly and 'close' several of her screens on the computer workstation that she was on at that time, which started 'alarm bells' ringing in my head because this seemed inappropriate for 'legitimate' work, but I could not prove anything at that time and as things became much more heavy towards me over the coming months and certain higher ranking Officers became more oppressive, I could not see how I could prove my suspicions, but I would still try and monitor this from a distance!

Looking back on things and seeing how you might have dealt with things differently is something that we all do from time to time and, as events rolled out, one scenario, screamed out to both my wife and I that Constable B.B. was in effect 'stalking' me!

We had been on a social function and when I say 'we', that was all the crime evaluators and I together with, later in the evening, my wife, and this was to celebrate a colleagues birthday so it was drinks and then on to a restaurant for a meal.
My wife joined us at the restaurant after the meal, together with two good friends of ours because we were going to move on and have a night out in the local town leaving the others there.

Whilst I was at the bar of the restaurant, another female colleague, whom I shall refer to as constable Barry, slightly worst for alcohol, approached me and said "you are a really nice bloke Mitchell and the best Sergeant I have ever worked with. If there is ever anything work related that you need to talk about, then don't take it home because your wife is such a lovely caring lady and shouldn't be hassled by your work, tell me and I am certain that it can be sorted out!"

This was a genuine comment made by a colleague who was aware of some of the battles I had fought and I took it in exactly the right context that it was intended.

My wife, who was also at the restaurant by now, also saw this as innocent but Constable B.B. on the other hand, took this opportunity to approach my wife and say "Don't worry, Mitchell is NOT having an affair with her, do you understand, he is NOT having an affair with her!" Constable B.B. emphasised the word NOT several times and knew EXACTLY what she was trying to do which upset my wife extremely and resulted in her going to the ladies room in tears!
Not satisfied with this, Constable B.B. then approached me and said "Mitchell, I think you had better go and see your wife because she thinks you are having an affair with (Constable Barry)!"

Well, as you can probably imagine, I was really astonished and concerned that my wife had become upset and couldn't understand why because I have never given her any reasons to doubt my fidelity and yet now, for reasons unknown to me at that precise time, she was upset and possibly in tears!

So I went and found her immediately and faced her crying and shouting "Do you know what (Constable B.B.) has just told me?"

At the same time, she lashed out at me with her arms and I asked what the hell was going on and causing her to react like this towards me.

When my wife explained, I then told her what constable B.B. had said to me and it was then that we both, shockingly, got our first thoughts about what this female was possibly and most deviously trying to do which was to split us up so that my wife would leave in tears and I may stay on to then, in constable B.B.'s thoughts, be vulnerable and open to being 'consoled' by her, a thought which, to be quite honest, makes my stomach churn even now, several years later and yet this was only the 'beginnings' of her 'master plan' so to speak!

Well, both of us were now 'aware' of what she was trying to do and so we made an 'overt' display of affection as we rejoined everyone in the

bar area thus 'snubbing' Constable B.B. and her attempts to drive us apart.
Shortly after this, my wife had her mobile phone stolen from off a table, quite coincidently /suspiciously, at the same time as when Constable B.B. decided to abruptly leave, however we could not positively identify the thief but the circumstantial evidence that presented itself after the event, well, I will let you make your own mind up!

You see, when we realised her phone was missing, I tried to ring it several times and it rang out until going to voicemail which happened several times until it was switched off by someone.

We called the Police and reported the crime, which was recorded correctly, but then, several days later, the mobile phone was returned back to the restaurant through the letter box, apparently by a woman who 'found it' in her hand bag, but, it had been smashed beyond repair!

Well, accidents do happen.......don't they?

Call me paranoid, but, as time passed, I began noticing Constable B.B. looking at my mobile phone if I was texting on it or looking at something in my pictures if I had them open (she unfortunately sat at the work station next to mine) and, on several occasions, my mobile went missing for a short period, only to reappear on my desk at a later time and eventually I kept it with me at all times and 'locked it' with a password because I suspected that she had been responsible although I could not prove this!

I also saw her on several occasions through my peripheral vision (out of the side of your eyes), looking over when my desk drawer was open to see what was inside and this began to play on my mind somewhat, but each time I turned around, she went back to her computer screen as if nothing had happened!

These were strange actions to say the least but I could do nothing whatsoever about it because no 'wrongdoing' had occurred.

I subsequently decided that I would 'remove myself' from my Godparent duties because I was becoming uneasy with the Officer and her behaviour!

When I told her this, let's just say that her demeanour became so different and she was 'hostile' towards me, but I did not feel the need to do anything further because I was, after all, the Sergeant and should unprofessionalism occur, well that was what the rank structure and regulations were there for and, at that time, I believed that this would suffice but how wrong I was!

Constable B.B. 'demanded', at a later date, that I have an affair with her which I obviously refused and could not believe the audacity of this individual because she was now becoming totally irrational and unprofessional which worried me.
One of my Federation Reps actually told me that I had been the only supervisor that they knew of who had actually stood up against Constable B.B. and her 'advances' and they felt that this was one of the reasons that she had become extremely hostile towards me, well, if that was the case, then I am proud of that fact and would never change!

I tried to treat all staff equally and fairly but I would not become a 'soft touch' and bend the rules for anyone, yet this is what Constable B.B. had wanted and she had a devious knack of exaggerating anything whatsoever and 'putting the tears on' to attract sympathy or deflect bad attention from her and yet, despite many, many, staff being aware of her manipulating ways, nobody ever did anything to stop it, apart from me and nobody ever sought to 'question' her ways and checks made on Police systems which, in my opinion from what I had observed, were dubious.

Acting D.C.I. Lewis had now become something of a 'puppet' for her and, if anything occurred that she was not happy with, she would go and see him and 'pull his strings' and then, surprisingly, shortly afterwards, either he or the female D.I. would intervene rightly or wrongly!

I strongly believe now, that Constable B.B. had decided that if I was not going to be like all her other supervisors and 'succumb' to her advances, especially because I believe she suspected that I was on to her corrupt ways, that she would do everything possible to destroy me and this was confirmed when she told me face to face "If you do not leave me alone I will create so much trouble and accusation that I will destroy you!"

Things came to a head in 2008 when Constable B.B. raised an issue about a serious crime in 'open office' which is how we sometimes worked (where you could run something past whoever was in the office at that time because several heads are better than one when looking at an issue) and myself and another evaluator gave advice to her but, despite this, Constable B.B. wanted to take other action and so I asked for the crime to be sent to me and I would endorse it accordingly as discussed, which was the correct course of action to take.

This was something that this Officer was repeatedly now doing, ignoring instructions from me as her Sergeant or advice from a colleague and trying to 'ride it out' her own way, subsequently causing more problems by giving wrong directions out to the Officer in the case and so I would have been neglecting my duty if I did not intervene!

The Officer then made an 'outburst' in the office accusing me of only intervening to 'justify' my being there which was totally unacceptable and then brought up previous 'upsets' that she had had with me (these were in fact quite legitimate challenges that I had made when I suspected that the Officer was abusing Police regulations and not carrying her work out professionally) and, because it was in 'open office' there were other staff present who looked a little awkward with the unfolding events, I suggested that this be taken 'elsewhere' to discuss the matter but Constable B.B. refused and so I continued in the presence of other staff to deal with the unprofessional behaviour which resulted in her abruptly leaving the office and not return for some time!
I since ascertained that she went to see the female D.I. and then acting D.C.I. Lewis, but that was the type of person she seemed to be, if she felt 'threatened', no matter how legitimate the challenge was, she would make a complaint (throw enough mud and eventually some should stick, as the saying goes!)

When she left the office I turned to the other staff members present and apologised that they had to witness such a confrontation and explained that I had no other option but to deal with it 'head on', which they did not disagree with.

Not surprisingly, after so many 'complaints' made by constable B.B. to her 'favoured' D.I. and acting D.C.I. I came under 'scrutiny' by them both regarding my 'welfare' which was somewhat coincidental because this was later on the same day that Constable B.B. had 'erupted' in front of other staff!

I was then 'summonsed' to see the Superintendent at that time, who I shall refer to as superintendent Dyke and as soon as I went into his office, I saw another Officer, an acting Ch. Insp. Referred to as Ch. Insp. Boyle And I soon ascertained that the meeting was to discuss 'concerns' raised.

It transpired that Constable B.B. had been 'working overtime' in her efforts to 'stitch me up' and had alleged that I had been extremely oppressive towards her and when I explained exactly what was occurring, both the senior Officers were satisfied that I was correct in my actions and did not need to pursue the matter any further, which was fine by me, but was most certainly not for Constable B.B.

The following day, another situation was brought to the fore by this Officer and another 'complaint' made by her to acting D.C.I. Lewis after she had 'stormed' out of the office accusing me of 'checking up' on her and when I attempted to pacify her with an explanation that, in fact, she was assuming something that was incorrect, she screamed at me "Bollocks", which is totally unacceptable behaviour and shocked other staff present in the office!

Acting D.C.I. Lewis was now looking for any reason whatsoever to remove me from my role, which, spookily enough, had only begun to happen after I had challenged him regarding the 'horse whip' conversation, but perhaps I was being paranoid? I don't think so, do you?

Anyway, I was again 'summonsed' to the Superintendents' office and, quite to my amazement, was told that they had arranged an 'urgent' appointment for me to see another force medical doctor concerning my 'welfare'!

I could not believe that one Officer, whose actions were dubious, could persuade these ranking Officers that I was 'attacking' her in the workplace and, more disturbingly, was 'abusing my authority' against her and that, it seemed, despite being able to 'evidence' many problems with her, they did not wish to listen or, in fact, examine the evidence that I had compiled.

It was almost as if they themselves were actually 'scared' of Constable B.B. and what she was capable of!

I even challenged Superintendent Dyke by asking if he felt that it was acceptable for an Officer to reply "Bollocks" to me or anyone else in 'open forum' and what would he do if I said it to him in front of other ranking Officers?
Needless to say, Supt. Dyke Chose to 'pass it over' and returned the conversation to being about me, which was a sign of my future and also of the corruption that was to follow from him and the acting D.C.I.

I attended the force doctors' appointment, as instructed and took with me my wife and my Fed Rep.
When I saw the Dr, whom I refer to as Dr Shackles, I was asked by him "Why are you here?" and so I explained what was happening and how disgusted and upset I was about my treatment and, after 'checking me over', the force Dr stated that all he could see in me was a conscientious, caring, genuine, honest Police Officer and that I should NOT let anything change this!

The following day, I returned to work and, as I came out of the lift to go to my office, I was 'greeted' by Supt. Dyke and requested to go down to his office where I saw that, yet again, there was Acting Ch. Insp. Boyle' in the office also and I knew, deep down, that these Officers had a 'hidden agenda' concerning me in mind.

I presented the Supt. with the report from the Dr I had seen and could see the expression of disappointment appear on his face because he had not got the result he obviously wanted and now my mind was racing with fear and distrust because something was happening and, no matter what I did, I could not seem to defend myself whatsoever at the hands of these ranking Officers, yet I had no idea what I was alleged to have done!

I could now obviously see that my time working in the crime evaluators' office was coming to an end through no fault of my own because I was instructed to remain at home until yet another case conference could be arranged for me to attend!

I would not, however, allow any 'foul play' prevent me from continuing my role as N.C.R.S. Sgt because I would be able to carry that out at any location and I most certainly would make serious complaints should anyone try to do that to me without a very, very, strong argument to justify that course of action, of which, unless there was to be even more lies and deceit from higher ranks, there was not one!

This was now having an extremely detrimental effect upon my family and my health and, as is always the case, 'rumour squads' would most definitely prevail, yet I complied because I had done nothing whatsoever wrong and had to now put all my faith in the experts who would be attending with me to 'fight my corner'!

My 'case conference' was held in October, somewhat 'expedited' by the 'organisational reps', and was led by supt. Dyke and Civilian Baders (no surprises there then!) and, despite my specifically stating that I did not want acting D.C.I. Lewis present because he was bias, they chose to bring him, which summed up their disregard to my position, but I did manage to ensure my wife, the Fed. Rep. and the Force Dr were present because, after all the treatment I had had to date, I suspected that this was going to get 'dirty' and it did!

I brought my own voice recorder to this meeting (which was something I now ALWAYS had with me and informed all present that it was for my own peace of mind due to my stress and anxiety and depression causing me to have short term memory loss.

Supt. Dyke and Acting D.C. I. Lewis objected to this and my Fed. Rep. made representation for me questioning, why.

At this time there was an atmosphere of 'animosity' which both my wife and I felt because they did not want me to audio record the conference in case, in Supt. Dykes own words, "IT COULD GET INTO THE WRONG HANDS!" which I could not understand his rational for same because it was after all, for my own reference and also protection as an accurate record.

What he was really concerned about, I later discovered, was that he did not want this and other matters ever to get into the public domain!

I had lost all trust in the Organisation again and was paranoid about intentions now.

I even suggested that I give it to the Fed Rep after the meeting, but civilian Baders, supt. Dyke and Acting D.C.I. Lewis were still not happy with this and I felt they were somewhat 'hostile' with their views.

Supt. Dyke stopped the conference and my wife and I were asked to wait outside!

Whilst out, civilian Baders went out of the building and returned sometime later, at which point my wife and I were asked back in (underhand conversations and arrangements had been occurring during this time and we both knew this by the way civilian Baders 'body language' was).

Upon returning into the office I was then informed, BEFORE I COULD RECORD MATTERS, that civilian Baders (H. R.), had liaised with the Attendance Management Unit and that audio recording was "not normal policy or procedure" and so Supt. Dyke stated "IT COULD NOT BE AUDIO RECORDED BY ME"!

Yet AGAIN, 'closing of ranks' was occurring where matters of my well being were concerned!

I was extremely unsettled by this and told them in no uncertain terms that under the Disability Discrimination Act (DDA), for which I was registered through my Force, this should be a 'Reasonable Adjustment' and so did the Fed. Rep. (This is all on audio tape because I wanted to ensure that their actions and demeanour were evidenced and so I placed it on and made them know that it was recording).

Supt. Dyke STILL REFUSED THIS and so, because of how I was now left to feel, attacked again by the Bosses, I looked at all three of the Organisational representatives and stated that Policy and Procedure were exactly that, Policy and Procedure, NOT law, but that the DDA WAS LAW and that they, whatever rank they held, are there to uphold the law, NOT MAKE OR BREAK IT, then I asked my Fed. Rep. to obtain legal advice for me, which he left the room to do and the meeting was again placed on 'hold'.

Supt Dyke , Acting D.C.I. Lewis and civilian Baders were obviously not happy about my stance which we could all see by their facial expressions, but I did not give a damn now, because they were being very negative and hostile towards me and I felt this was more corrupt ways coming from them!

After legal advice was taken, it was held that it was a 'reasonable adjustment' under the DDA, if it was on record that I suffered memory loss.

Supt. Dyke was quick to ask the Force Dr if this was the case and Dr Slade confirmed it was.

Reluctantly, they 'allowed' the case conference to be audio recorded but I still felt a heavy negative attitude toward me.
I served on all present, a set of papers that I had prepared that illustrated how I felt by the way I was being treated, but these were put to one side by the bosses as if "so what".

At the end of the conference, because I had been told I was not going back to the Police Station where I had been stationed at that time (despite Constable B.B. remaining there even though she had been 'fuelling the fire for the bosses with her concerns), I suggested that I go to a station which was near my home as opposed to them deciding further afield to do my NCRS Sgt role although Supt. Dyke took away my supervisory role over the crime evaluators 'temporarily'.

During a 'break' in the case conference, as I was about to leave for some fresh air, Acting D.C.I. 'N.O' looked directly at me as soon as everyone else had left the room and I was about to and said "You're very good at rebutting accusations made against you aren't you Mitchell!"

Well, I was took aback by his 'devious' nature and comment and just walked out, but made sure my wife knew what he had just said!

This was a 'one word against the other' scenario with him again, just like the 'whip' conversation and so I knew that he would deny it and try to make me look, like him, devious and I was not going to allow him the satisfaction and lower myself to his level by doing so!

Moving me to another station was a direct discriminatory act towards me because I WAS BEING MOVED AND CONSTABLE B.B. REMAINED AT WHERE SHE WAS!

I still felt that this was only the 'tip of the iceberg' and could not understand why the audio recording had become such an issue other than it prevented them from 'brow beating' me and becoming oppressive.

So, after this meeting, I was 'transferred' temporarily to a station near to my home, BUT, I was not going to be 'silenced' or closed down by oppression and harassment and, in fact, over the next chapter, you will see so much 'corruption', lies and deceit, I believe it will astonish you!

CHAPTER THIRTEEN – CORRUPTION WITHIN.

Corruption comes across in two main forms namely:-

What an Individual or Organisation says

And

What an Individual or Organisation does.

This is no different in the Police Force and is 'fed down' from higher positions sometimes in policies or procedures, sometimes in legislation or 'guidance' documents and sometimes by word of mouth!

If things that are not morally right or are potentially illegal are not challenged, then you, the individual, become tarnished with the same corruption which, at first, seems wrong, but, by doing nothing about it, it becomes 'the norm' for you and you no longer can see clearly what is right or wrong, no 'black or white', just a dull 'grey'!

Well I certainly WAS NOT going to allow that to occur where I was concerned, BUT, yet again, I would suffer harshly because of my stance!

I shall start, whilst it is still fresh in my memory, with my previous encounter outside the lift doors with Supt. Dyke' when I presented him with an official Drs report which stated that I was fine to continue with my role on the Lima.

After handing this to him, on his request, I was NEVER to see that again because it was not what he wanted to read and, after 'perusing' the report, he took it to 'photocopy' after which, it then, unsurprisingly, 'disappeared'!

Constable B.B. was later to make a statement which contained lies, concerning an allegation of a serious criminal offence, BUT, did not wish to pursue that, merely to 'bring it to the attention' of my senior Officers and so, on the advice of the Federation, I compiled a 25 page report outlining what I knew of her dishonest and discreditable actions in the 'belief' that this would be investigated, only for her to then, several days later, make a SECOND statement now wishing to make a formal criminal complaint and contained within this second statement, she had attempted to 'account' for every point that I had brought up in my report!

How did that happen, you may perhaps ask? Well, there is only one logical explanation for that which was that someone within the 'organisation' had provided her with A FULL COPY of my report and directed / advised her what to do about it!

This is not the correct course of action and, in my opinion, is another example of corruption, because my report contained allegations of serious fraud, discreditable conduct and sexual harassment by the Constable as well as potential fraudulent actions by some of the crime evaluation staff and by allowing her to see this, she would be able to attempt to 'cover her tracks', which she tried and, shockingly, seemed to be supported by those civilians and Police Officers in positions of power to do so!

I know this because, after my arrest and subsequent exoneration, I obtained, quite legitimately, through the solicitors representing me, both copies of her statements, yet none of my allegations, of which I had proof from both witnesses and documents, were ever investigated as they should have been and this only gave Constable B.B. a feeling of being 'untouchable', something which, for a corrupt Police Officer to believe, is extremely dangerous indeed!

I also later submitted a further report concerning a serious criminal offence committed by Constable B.B. of 'Perverting the Course of Justice', yet nothing from this was ever investigated until, at a much later date, once I had retired, I made a formal complaint as Mr Spence, now a civilian and they even attempted to 'brush this under the carpet' and do minimal actions with it.

I therefore appealed this to the IPCC (Independent Police Complaints Commission) who, as it says in their title, are totally independent of the Police and they upheld my appeal.
Statistically, from what I am led to believe, the IPCC only uphold 20% of appeals that are made to them and I strongly suspect that this is what

my previous Force had hoped would occur, but that was not to be and the IPCC subsequently directed them to reinvestigate the matter properly and not as they had attempted to do previously, which I strongly suspect seriously annoyed them yet again, but I was not and still am not, someone who, when something is wrong or corrupt, will simply move on or put my head in the sand as the saying goes.

This direction meant that my previous Force had no choice because they themselves were now being watched by a power much greater than themselves and to whom they were accountable.

The IPCC only normally oversee matters that could show serious neglect or blame on a Police Force such as deaths in Police custody, a fatal or serious Police pursuit accident or fatal or serious shooting amongst a few that I can mention and so, you can probably see from this, the IPCC realised, quite correctly, that my complaint involved such criminal matters that fell into their 'remit' and so, the once oppressive Police Force who tried to do so much damage to me, were now the 'prey' of something bigger than them and quite rightly so.

I will expand on the final results of this in the final chapter of this book, but suffice to say that they, my old Force, still felt that they could take their time, presumably so that I became ill, so much so that I may just withdraw my complaint before any conclusion.

I did suffer due to this, but kept at them to ensure that, to the best of my capability, as a civilian, the investigation was carried out to the full.

As a result of my standing up for truth and justice, I had to endure the unsettling experience of watching a very serious and dangerous criminal drive very slowly past my home address one evening and, whilst doing so, stare into my home at both my wife and I!

I am not someone who is easily frightened and so I made a point of going to my window and staring back at him and his 'associate' as they drove past, turned around and drove past again because, if this was going to 'get personal' then I would put all my morals aside and face them both head on.

I knew that this had to be connected to Constable B.B. because she had previously made it known to anyone she felt 'threatened' by (including myself), that she had worked for a well known criminal solicitors prior to joining the Police and could 'call upon favours owed' at any time to 'put people down' or 'settle scores', however I am also the type of person who will do whatever it takes to protect my family and property, something which, only recently, has finally been acknowledged as a Citizens right in society to do so providing that this is, given all the information available, 'reasonable in the circumstances'.

Despite my making an official complaint regarding the latter 'drive by', I was ignored and it was treated as 'not important' and so I was left with no other option than to take my Police issue 'airwaves' radio home with me when not in work and my family were under my instructions to call 999 and also me should anything more sinister occur!

Whilst working, from a distance at another station, I ensured that I kept a look at what the evaluators were doing whilst I was not physically present to supervise them and was quite shocked with what I found.

All work was carried out 'electronically' because crimes would be input onto a main computer to be progressed or filed and, as well as this, the evaluators would have to 'log in' to access data, which then illustrated to me what time they started, had breaks and subsequently finished their tour of duty, which should have been 8 hours, but, as I soon found out, this was not the case!

I uncovered that, whilst there was no direct supervision in their office, they were starting later than they should, having 'extended' refreshment periods (which are normally NO MORE than 45 minutes yet these were becoming 1 hour, 1.5 hours and, on some occasions, 2 hours!) and also finishing earlier than they should, in some cases, several hours earlier and yet NO ONE WAS DOING ANYTHING ABOUT IT!

I even discovered that one Constable, yes, Constable B.B. had taken HALF A DAY OFF and there was no documentation to allow this, ever submitted by her.
If that is not dishonest, then what is?

So, I took it upon myself to compile all the information I had uncovered and place it into a 'costing' factual document including any requests for time off to account for when they had started late or finished early and you might be surprised, not, to find that these were NON EXISTENT!

I attached copies of ALL requests for annual leave or 'cumulative' time off (C.T.O) for the full period covered to illustrate to the senior ranks, that something was untoward because, if you uncover dishonesty or corruption, well you must be able to 'evidence' this and I was making damn sure that I could!

When I did this, I covered the period between October 2008 and December 2008 and found there were over 104 hours unaccounted for.

That is thirteen days, working eight hour tours of duty, where officers had potentially taken time off without permission.

There was only one Constable who did not have any doubtful periods whatsoever and he was the one who had become disabled due to hospital operation mistakes, yet he ALWAYS, worked his full hours, took less than 45 minutes for his refreshment period and, from the moment he sat down at his workstation to the moment he finished to go home, his 'crime screens' and transactions were busy and correct.
They also worked at a separate station to the others and I have so much respect for them because they were honest, professional, genuine, and, despite all their disabilities, they ALWAYS put the public and colleagues before themselves.

They were a selfless person and A GOOD COP!

So, as you can see from the above figures, they realised, or so they thought, that without a supervisor present in the office, they could be a 'law unto their own', but I was not going to allow that to happen and, unless these 'anomalies' could be explained, each and every one of those above SHOULD have been dealt with either under discipline regulations or, should it be shown to be the case with dishonesty involved, dealt with AS CRIMINALS!

Remember my quoting my belief of 'a good days work for a good days pay' earlier in the book?

Well I stood by that moral because the public should receive the service they expect from public servants, as the Police are, shouldn't they?

So what happened as a result of my highlighting this you may be asking?

Well, I will explain now.

Another 'case conference' was arranged for me to attend at a later date and, because I had audio recorded the meeting on the last occasion, for this one, civilian Baders and Supt. Dyke had other ideas and I believe, thought that they were being smart because they brought official tape recording equipment with them, the type you would use in a crime enquiry, so that, in their own words, I would not need to use mine and the recordings would be kept safe and secure!

These recordings were kept so safe and secure that, when I asked for copies of them at a later date, they had been initially 'misplaced' and then, presumably after a 'rethink', they DENIED the existence of any recordings and civilian Baders emphasised this several times to me!

I had wanted these for potential legal action that I may have taken against them and I believe that they realised the content of the meeting might not show them or the 'Organisation' in good light, well if that is not corrupt, then what is?

So, back to the resultant proceedings from my document release, I received the biggest warning that I have ever received in my entire career from Supt. Dyke who said along the lines of 'if I had been in internal affairs (investigation of Police Officers), then he would have told me that I had done a fantastic job in my investigation, BUT, I WAS NOT AND HAD BEEN TOLD THAT I WAS NOT RESPONSIBLE FOR SUPERVISING THE CRIME EVALUATORS AT THAT PARTICULAR TIME AND HAD GONE AGAINST A DIRECT INSTRUCTION GIVEN!'

I did answer back to him that AT NO TIME WHATSOEVER had I been exactly told that and I had merely been told that I was to continue my

NCRS role at another location which I did, but that as part of that role, I had come across the information and decided to 'monitor' it a little more closely.

Whether I should or should not have done so is something that you, the reader, will have to decide in your own mind, but as far as I was concerned, If I uncovered things that were dishonest, then as a Police Officer and decent human being, if it is within my power to do so, then I must bring this out into the open and it MUST be investigated!

I stipulated that I wanted to know what the outcome of the 'investigation' was and Supt. 'R.S' assured me that I would be informed, but, as was regularly occurring now, I was not and strongly believe that it NEVER WAS INVESTIGATED!

My rationale for this conclusion was that if there had been an investigation, some very close colleagues of mine who were trying to 'keep me in the loop' would have got to find out and let me know and, of course, I would have been the main witness because I instigated it in the first place and would have to, at some point, have given my evidence either at a disciplinary hearing against any Officer suspected or at a criminal trial should that have occurred, but I did not and so corruption was covered over by, in my opinion, more corruption but by senior ranks and a civilian H.R. boss!

It seemed now that, no matter what misdemeanours or dishonest actions I may bring to their attention, NOTHING would be done about it.

I continued my role in the professional capacity that I held but came across more and more 'opposition' which I shall explain further now.

I was 'approached' by another Inspector who was in the 'fast track' promotion system and I was asked to contact 5 'customers' (members of the public but now called customers) and ensure that these were people who had received an excellent service from the local Police on the Lima and 'invite' them to come to the station to be part of a meeting with the Police Authority, the Chief Constable or representative and members of command (the Chief Superintendent, Superintendents and a couple of Chief Inspectors) at a specific time and date to give their 'feedback' on the way they had been dealt with.

This request was on behalf of Supt. Dyke and the reason they wanted people who had had a good level of service was obvious to me and probably to you.

It was so that they all looked 'excellent' in the eyes of the Police Authority and Chief Constable and as far as I was concerned, in my opinion, this was yet more corrupt ways and I wanted none of that, so I took things into my own hands and, yes, I complied with the 'request', BUT, on my terms which I will explain now!

I did carry out their 'instructions' and contacted members of the public except that I made a point of contacting those who were 'known' to the Police (had criminal records or cautions) but who had been victims of crime also and explained fully why I had contacted them and that this was their opportunity to sit in a meeting with influential persons and tell them EXACTLY how good or, as was most probably going to be the case, how bad the service they had received was.

I even had some of these people thinking I was 'setting them up' initially but I built up their trust and they soon came 'onside' after I had explained my rationale because they too did not agree with corruption and saw the initial request for 'good people' as 'bent'.

I did not get asked to carry out that 'task' again and to be quite honest, didn't care because, as far as I was concerned, I had done what was right and proper and it was very much a bonus to perhaps 'upset' the bosses by having done so!

We hear, almost every day, how crime has reduced and the streets are a safer for us all and this obviously reflects upon the Police Forces performance, but how much of this is true and how much of this is simply 'spin'?

Well, I would like to enlighten you, the reader, as to some of the 'experiences' I had with what, in my opinion, I can only describe as 'figure fiddling' by ranks in power on the Lima Division!

I would 'oversee' incident logs and crimes connected to those as I have previously mentioned and act accordingly to ensure things were as they should be.

If a crime or crimes can be 'reclassified' to a lesser one, then obviously the more serious crimes were being reduced and so, statistics released to the public domain would show a 'fall' in the more serious categories, BUT, this was not necessarily the true picture and should not have been happening!

I 'monitored' an incident where two males had fallen out and had a fight in the street which resulted in one 'winning' and one 'losing', the normal outcome of any fight you would say, but on this occasion, the 'loser' chose to go to his home and return brandishing a metal hammer which he then attacked the 'winner' with, subsequently splitting his head open and inflicting 'really serious bodily harm' upon him.

The Police were called to the scene and, quite correctly, a crime was recorded for 'Grievous Bodily Harm with intent, (section 18 wounding) (because the 'loser' had formed the intent in his mind to go and get the hammer and then hit the 'winner' over the head with it to cause serious harm). This was the most serious of the crimes below murder or manslaughter or attempting either of those.

Offences against the person are placed into the following categories:-

1) Common Assault (a slap to the face causing reddening but nothing more)
2) Actual Bodily Harm (section 47 assault) (severe bruising or more serious cuts etc)
3) Grievous Bodily Harm (Section 20 wounding) (really serious bodily harm such as serious broken bones or wounds caused by a knife etc)
4) Grievous Bodily Harm with INTENT (Section 18 wounding) (really serious bodily harm or wounds as at (3) above but with the most important aspect of INTENT i.e. you made your mind up prior to committing the crime, that you were going to inflict serious harm on another.

These can be readily viewed on the Governments web site under 'Home Office Counting Rules' or if you use a 'search engine' then search with the heading 'Home Office Counting Rules' and, should you choose to read them, they are somewhat 'enlightening' BUT, you will need some considerable time to 'read and digest' these 'public' documents!

Obviously, after the above you have murder and manslaughter and attempts to commit those, but for the above incident, the crime submitted was correct as a section 18 wounding and was N.C.R.S. compliant, that was, of course, until C.I.D. bosses intervened and attempted to have the crime REDUCED in its category!

I further intervened with the 'instructions' that were being given to the reporting Officer regarding the crime and ensured that my knowledge and guidance was written upon the incident log which was a 'disclosable' document at any court proceedings and this caused a 'tit for tat' scenario to emerge between myself and the C.I.D. bosses, all written up on the log!

The Officer was being instructed to submit a lesser crime for (2) above which was totally wrong and annoyed me extremely because the bosses had not even looked at (3) which, although better than (2) was still wrong.

I could see through the whole situation and knew that C.I.D. did not want a more serious crime submitted because they could have been left with it 'undetected' and that would reflect badly upon the D.I. and Acting D.C.I. Lewis but that was the correct way to comply with N.C.R.S. and so I stood my ground with it to the point of being 'advised' on the log by the C.I.D. bosses to 'revert from writing upon this incident log because it is disclosable at court'!

Eventually I decided to forward the whole matter to the Force Crime Registrars' Office with my views and, quite correctly, they concurred with my advice and eventually the correct crime was recorded and remained to be investigated.

As referred to above, most crimes are recorded in accordance with what are called 'Home Office Counting Rules' and these come from the Home Office and stipulate the way a crime or crimes should be recorded, but they do have their 'flaws' or 'grey areas' and I most certainly do not personally agree with how many crimes are categorised.

You see, if I were staying at your house and you were burgled, but in the process of your burglary, the offenders stole my motor car to transport your property, then you would think that there are two crimes here, a burglary against you and a theft of motor vehicle against me, wouldn't you?

Well that is how it used to be when I first became a Police Officer in 1985 and obviously the volume of crimes reported was huge, but surely that was right because if you reported a crime, then a crime should be recorded as it was and not 'amended' and the numbers of crimes should stand as committed and not 'included' in others shouldn't they?

Not anymore, and this is where the 'statistics' are able to show 'crime is reducing', when, perhaps, it may be arguable!

For the burglary scenario above, instead of two crimes being submitted, there would now only be one, a burglary but contained within that crime would be reference to my theft of motor vehicle and so now you can possibly see how TWO CRIMES BECOME ONE!

Is that right or is that wrong?

Well I will leave you to make your own opinion up of that, but this is the way it now is as resources deplete and financial budgets shrink, but IS IT RIGHT?

In another statistic, a certain type of vehicle crime is 'un-disclosed' which means that it is recorded as a crime, BUT, it is not required to be included in the vehicle crime statistics!

The crime I refer to is 'vehicle interference' and a scenario that would fit this is where I enter your vehicle and attempt to break your steering column, obviously to steal your car or else why would I do such a thing?

I have committed damage to your car in doing so, but I did not manage to steal it so you may think then that a crime for attempted theft of motor vehicle would be submitted, but this is not the case and the argument against that crime is that 'you cannot prove the mens-rea (state of mind) of the offender at that time and so the 'vehicle interference' crime would be submitted, not even a damage to motor vehicle because, as with the attempt theft, that is 'disclosable' in statistics and so the value damage is incorporated into the vehicle interference and, not surprisingly, where a crime has been committed, it becomes 'invisible' and so now vehicle crime is reducing!

I am sure that you can imagine, with guidelines such as these and also C.I.D. fighting against serious wounding and other crimes being submitted as illustrated above, then it 'casts a shadow' on the 'statements' or 'spin' that come out periodically concerning crime reducing and I for one, most certainly do not believe it is accurate!

I had a major disagreement concerning another incident, a serious crime of attempt abduction, with C.I.D. because they initially REFUSED to allow a crime to be recorded and this was, as I understand, on the advice of either the Acting D.C.I. Lewis Or their D.I. and I fought long and hard over this, believe me.

Again, I had been monitoring the incident logs and saw that two young boys had been approached by two men in a white lorry who had slowed down to 'ask directions' from them and, from the accounts given, when the boys were close enough to the passenger, he tried to drag them into the lorry!

This is a serious incident and, although the boys were only young, perhaps 10 or 11, they should have been believed by the Police, but this was not the case, until I became involved.

Both boys had run to one of their homes and informed the adult present who had then, whilst the Police were being called, taken them out in her vehicle to see if they could find the offenders, which, in my opinion, was the best course of action to take because then perhaps a registration number could be obtained and, in these days of mobile phones, a call could be made to the Police again whilst, perhaps, following the lorry.

Unfortunately the lorry was not found, but good descriptions were given of the vehicle and a little towards the offenders.
Either way, a crime should be submitted for the attempt abduction and, should it be ascertained at a later date, that this was not exactly the

correct version of events, the crime could be 'written off', but at least press releases could be made appealing for information and, most importantly, this could prevent a second, more successful attempt being made!

Items like this are now 'shared' on social media sites very quickly by the Police now which is at least a move in the right direction where crime prevention and detection is concerned.

C.I.D. would have none of this and, despite the reporting Officer having commenced local enquiries, were reluctant to take it any further which frustrated the Officer reporting extremely and so they contacted me for advice (the reporting Officer, not C.I.D. who did not want to 'lower themselves' to that).

I backed the Officer completely and then commenced writing upon the incident log, again much to the annoyance of C.I.D!

I referred the matter to the Force Crime Registrar who again, concurred with my views but still C.I.D. did not wish such a serious crime to be recorded, they were looking at 'downgrading' the whole incident log to nothing more than a 'suspicious circumstances' which was as much use as a 'chocolate fireguard'!

Two days elapsed before they eventually submitted a crime report for attempt abduction and this was, if I recall correctly, only because I had updated them with information about a possible SECOND attempt in a neighbouring Police area with the same offenders and vehicle which I think, caused them a little unease but, I am glad to say, brought around the correct procedure and investigation.

It was, and still is, ridiculous to think that a crime or crimes are either not being reported or are being downgraded purely and simply because:-

   a) The Police want to appear as though they are winning the fight against crime
   And

b) The Political powers that be want to be able to utilise these 'improved' statistics to win votes!

Where does the safety and well being of you and me, the general public come into this equation?

So, you can probably see, from the small picture I have portrayed in this chapter, there was a considerable amount of what I believed was corruption, lies and deceit going on and so, when it came to my next appraisal (yearly and half yearly reports on an individuals' performance), you may not be surprised that, yet again, Acting D.C.I. Lewis attacked me and, when I challenged him about this, he then LIED and attempted to place the blame on the then female D.I.!

I will explain more for you.

At the time, I was due to have my 'interim' appraisal which is the one you have half way through the year and for this appraisal, the ONLY line manager that is involved is your IMMEDIATE RANK ABOVE YOU, thus, a Constable has a Sergeant reporting and a Sergeant has an Inspector reporting.

Straight forward you might think, but not in my case, well why should it be?

After all, I did not 'sing the Organisational song' and was 'trouble' because I was honest!

So, when my appraisal came around, I was initially shocked, though not totally surprised, to find that it was the WORST APPRAISAL I had been given in all my service and, spookily enough, ACTING D.C.I. Lewis HAD TAKEN A MAJOR PART IN WRITING AND COMMENTING UPON IT!

Contained within the 'interim appraisal' was a sheet labelled 3 of 6, on which Acting D.C.I. Lewis Slandered my 'mental health' not once but on 4 occasions and so, probably expected by them, I OBJECTED STRONGLY to this!

What they had not expected, was how far I would take this matter and so I submitted a 'complaint' and also endorsed the appraisal, which I refused to sign, that if he were so correct in his comments, then he MUST EVIDENCE THEM, which obviously he could not and I also challenged why he, the Acting D.C.I. had become involved in an appraisal that should have only had the female D.I. compiling!

The response from him was simple, yet unfortunately for him, flawed, and that was that the 'note' contained within my appraisal was not meant to be included and was only for the female D.I. to see, for 'reference' purposes!

When I demanded to know why it was on official documentation for appraisals AND was listed as page 3 of 6, well, he could not answer and I was told that he had stated the D.I. was at fault because it should not have been included and he would 'advise her' accordingly.

Another 'closing of ranks' example, however, this was not going to go away because I would make damn sure of that and again challenged him under the D.D.A. to 'evidence' further, which obviously, he could not!

Soon after this I was informed by Supt. Dyke that this appraisal 'was a mistake' and it would be 'removed' as obsolete and a new one would be compiled.
Well I was expecting a 'heads together' session and subsequent BAD APPRAISAL which could be used against me in any 'unsatisfactory performance' proceedings, yet was astonished with what I in fact received!

My appraisal was nothing but complement after complement and one of the best I had ever received, but it meant nothing to me other than this was proof of how 'low' these corrupt ranks would go to try and remove me from service and I held it in the contempt it deserved, merely a 'sweetener' to knock me off the scent so to speak!

I was then informed by my D.I. whom I shall refer to as D.I. 'V.W' that, as far as the 'time and motion' study was concerned, (because I had directly challenged her that I suspected it had NEVER been looked into despite 'promises' from supt. Dyke'), If I was 'checking up' on staff working hours, then I would also be 'accountable' and this was said, I believe, as a 'threat'!

My response was simple, I offered her ALL my pocket note books to illustrate my honesty and Integrity but, not surprisingly, she declined my offer.

The most sinister and malicious act of corruption as far as I was concerned occurred when I had seen my regular Force Dr, Dr Slade. He then reported back to the effect that I was 'progressing well and should be left alone to continue in my current role'.
This was placed upon an official medical document and forwarded to Force H.R. as well as Division and I also received a copy.

I was not surprised to find out, directly from the Force Dr, a Dr of many, many years in general practise and then working with the Police, that he had received 'strong advice' from Force H.R. and they had attempted to apply 'pressure' to him to make him 'rethink' his expert medical advice and change it to what was really wanted by them, obviously with an ulterior motive of looking at dismissing me from my career!

In his own words, they had said they were 'deeply concerned with his recommendations and advised him strongly to change these more in line with their own observations' as well as, what I saw as the biggest insult that they could give the Dr, which was that they 'felt he had poor managerial and people management skills' and recommended that he attend a 'developmental' course for this to be addressed!

I could not believe how serious this was becoming against me until I heard this directly and, at a later date, through the Freedom of Information and Data Protection Acts, I paid a fee and applied for all documentation, e mails, medical records / advice etc concerning me throughout the Force which would cover this area also but, when I received the paperwork, of which there was a large amount, it had all been 'sanitised' (where they block out anything that they feel is not relevant OR, although they would never admit it, anything that may INCRIMINATE them) and, surprise, surprise, the e mail between the head of Force H.R. and Dr Slade had been sanitised heavily throughout!

Dr. Slade had refused totally to change anything he had written about me and I actually apologised to him for being 'dragged into my fight', to which he remarked that he knew how genuine and decent I was and that nothing would make him change his expert medical advice concerning me and even told me that, should the 'Organisation' continue in its harassment, he would simply 'walk' because he did not need the role and was financially secure but continued doing what he did 'to help the Police out'!

I had and still have so much respect for Dr Slade because he was a genuine professional man with, in my own opinion, plenty of inner strength and courage.

I truly hope that at some point, Dr Slade reads this book and if he does, I just want to say "Thank you"!

CHAPTER FOURTEEN – MY RETURN TO THE EVALUATION OFFICE.

In February 2009 I had a new D.I. whom I shall refer to as D.I. Vickery and it was decided that I was to return to the evaluation office for 3 days per week.
When I did, I found that all my reference papers that were fixed onto the wall at the side of my desk were gone and my desk had been cleared, the items having been placed in a corner store area!
This gave me the feeling of not belonging and also that some individual(s) had believed I was not returning despite knowing this had been temporary from the outset.

Had I done such an act, then that would have been seen to be 'bullying' or 'harassment' yet someone had done this to me and none of my supervisors had chosen to act on it to prevent same (or chose to ignore it).

Due to a decision made by D.I. Vickery that he would deal with any issues regarding staff, Constable B.B. felt she was 'untouchable' and this she 'overtly' displayed whilst other staff were around by being somewhat arrogant towards me with her comments.

When my Fed. Rep. and D.I. Vickery told staff that I was returning, Constable B.B. was the only one who showed concern and 'kicked off' with them saying that I was 'out to get her' and that there were 'many ways to skin a cat'!
I received this information directly from my Fed. Rep. who advised me to 'look over my shoulder' where she was concerned.

Shortly afterwards, in September 2009 I had a meeting with D.I. Vickery to give me feedback from my return to the office because obviously Constable B.B. was present there and, not surprisingly, I was informed that she had made another complaint that I was ignoring her and talking to other staff.

I offered to speak to her regarding this because the matter to which she referred had been a conversation between two other staff members and me regarding their work, thus not relevant to Constable B.B.

I spoke to the Officer and other staff at the next available date when they were all in and Constable B.B. then made a further complaint that I had been derogatory towards her!

This now seemed to be her way again to try and remove me by complaints or concerns because in her eyes, it had worked previously and bosses had sided with her and dealt with me incorrectly!

Constable B.B. also caused unrest in the office with her arrogance and derogatory attitude and comments yet, no matter what I told the bosses about this, it was cast aside.

I was now also facing an internal investigation because Constable B.B. had made an allegation that I was 'bullying her'!

What else was this Officer capable of and how long would it be before someone in the organisation, other than me, would see her for what she actually was, a deceitful, dishonest and, as I suspected, a corrupt Police Officer.

Mediation was offered to both of us (this is where the two parties sit down together with a third 'independent' person and try to resolve any issues that had caused the problems) and I accepted this offer.

Constable B.B. had obviously thought that I would refuse, but why should I because I had done nothing whatsoever wrong!
As soon as she was told I had accepted, SHE PULLED OUT OF THE PROCESS!

That action alone should have given a clear picture of the Officers' intent and demeanour, but nobody commented upon it apart from my Federation Representative who knew all about her 'history' with anyone who she saw as a 'threat' or who did not accept her advances!

On 28/04/09 I went into work and couldn't take all that had been happening to me anymore. I felt unwell, heavily depressed, stressed and as if I had a noose around my neck going tighter!

I thus rang my G.P to make an urgent appointment and also Occupational Health because I was going to report sick.

The Force Medical Officer, Dr Slade agreed and fully supported me in my actions taken due to the way I was feeling and not being supported or listened to by Command.

After only two months back in the evaluators' office, here I was, very ill but this time removing myself from the environment before more excuses/complaints could be made and the 'powers that be' use the opportunity' to take matters out of my control again!

Whilst I was at my G.Ps surgery I got a call from my Fed. Rep. that Constable B.B. had now made serious criminal allegations against me and that the Foxtrot Division (where I began my career) were going to arrest me.

<u>I felt physically sick, my knees buckled and I ended up sat on the floor outside my G.P's in tears.</u>

My whole family, career and life were now being threatened by a corrupt Officers' deceit and lies and yet again the Organisation and the Lima Division had listened to her and not me despite my having submitted a report about Constable B.B. perverting the Course of Justice and my Fed. Rep.
Having sent a report to the Chief Inspector on the Lima (who had been present and aware of all matters throughout most of my ordeal), yet we were both ignored and unsupported!

It transpired that, in March 2009, Constable B.B. made a statement against me of a criminal nature, but refused to proceed with it, merely 'bringing it to the attention of senior Officers' and then, AFTER I had submitted my report concerning her, the SECOND statement was made now wishing to prosecute.

This set of allegations were 'historic' and these are very dangerous because they are extremely hard to disprove, yet easy to allege and when I say 'historic', Constable B.B. was making up lies about a social meeting FIFTEEN MONTHS EARLIER and what should have been even more obvious that it was lies was that MY WIFE HAD BEEN PRESENT THE

WHOLE TIME and, should I have committed the sickening allegations Constable B.B. was making, then why were they not made ON THE DATE OR SHORTLY AFTERWARDS?

I know exactly why this deceitful, corrupt Officer was making these allegations now and that was because she had a very good idea that I was on the trail of her corruption and, as I knew, needed just a little more time to act and obtain the evidence against her, so what better way to prevent this other than taking desperate action which would result in my removal completely!

I was never suspended from duty throughout the whole ordeal which is normal procedure where serious criminal complaints are made, so that in itself speaks volumes as I am sure you will agree.

I wrote the below poem concerning Constable B.B. and called it "A Cautious Tale to Bear in Mind"

"Beware of those you call a friend,
With their tales of woe that never end!

Trust only those who share your life,
Your relatives, sons and daughters,
But especially your husband or wife!

For all humans, they have a price,
Your name could be next when they throw the dice!

A genuine friend is there for you,
With no ulterior motives when you're down and you're blue.

The Dark Angel has many a cunning disguise,
To fool all of those who think they are wise!

So take heed of this poem,
Read it all take your time.....

**Because before you know it,
You could be next in its line!**

CHAPTER FIFTEEN – THE DARK TIMES AND THE CORRUPTION CONTINUES

I was now to enter a very dark time of my life that I will never forget and for which I still suffer the effects of today.

The person that I was will never return and my trust has been eroded completely!

Having been an honest person all my life and an honest Police Officer throughout my career, to now be treated as a criminal suspect was extremely traumatic for me!

The day of my arrest was a date that I will never forget because I was travelling to the Foxtrot Division with my Federation Representative, to be arrested and have my liberty taken from me for the next 6 hours and 40 minutes and that feeling is something that will forever be with me until I depart this life!

I remember vividly being placed under arrest by a female Detective Constable and then being escorted through the secure doors that I was familiar with from when, in my career, I had arrested suspects and also been a Custody Sergeant and they held no fear for me then, but now, I was like a lamb being taken to slaughter, totally helpless and frightened, yes, frightened because I was innocent but being treated by all concerned as 'guilty until proven guilty' and all I could sense was extreme numbness both physically and mentally and the only thoughts I had were how had it come to this and why?

I was placed before the Custody Sergeant, a man whom I immediately recognised from when I worked together with him when we were both Constables and who immediately recognised me and with a somewhat shocked expression asked me what I was doing there to which I replied, almost in tears," you tell me!"

The next action took me completely by surprise and that was the Detectives' grounds for arrest!

I will explain what is required under section 110(5) of the Serious Organised Crime and Police Act 2005 (SOCAPA):-

The above section of legislation lists all the reasons for which at least one MUST be shown to be NECESSARY to make any arrest LAWFUL namely –

- A) Name – suspects name cannot be ascertained or there is doubt that a name given by the suspect is correct.

- B) Address – The suspects address cannot be ascertained or there is doubt that the address is correct and in any case, the address MUST be suitable for a summons to be served (where a suspect is either personally served with a notice compelling them to attend a given court at a specific time and date to answer charges brought against them or where the summons can be left with a third party).

- C) Arrest is NECESSARY to prevent the suspect from –

    - i) causing physical injury to themselves or another,
    - ii) suffering physical injury (if not arrested),
    - iii) causing loss of or damage to property,
    - iv) committing an offence against public decency (for example indecent exposure),
    - v) Causing an unlawful obstruction of the highway.

- D) To protect a child or other vulnerable person from the suspect.

- E) To allow the prompt and effective investigation of the offence or the conduct of the person.

    Effective Investigation includes –

- Belief that the suspect has made a false statement,

- Belief that he/she has made a false statement that cannot be readily verified,
- The suspect has presented false evidence,
- The suspect may steal or destroy evidence,
- The suspect may make contact with co-suspects or conspirators,
- The suspect may intimidate, threaten or make contact with witnesses.

When considering an arrest in connection with an indictable offence (one that can ONLY be tried at CROWN COURT) and there is an operational need –

- To enter and search any premises controlled by the suspect,
- To search the suspect,
- To prevent contact with others,
- To take fingerprints, footwear impressions, samples (intimate or non intimate) or photograph the suspect,
- To ensure compliance with mandatory drug testing requirements.

F) To prevent any prosecution being hindered by the disappearance of the suspect.

The arresting officer MUST specifically state which of the above make the arrest of a suspect necessary and proportionate and in my case, this was NOT done AND none of the above were relevant to me, after all, I was aware that I was to be arrested and when I had my mobile phone seized by the detectives investigating, I actually explained to them that the phone to which they referred, was in the possession of my wife to ensure that it was available to them for examination because I had, only two days previously, received a new phone upgrade and was in the process of transferring all my contacts to my new one and that they could take possession of it whenever they wanted to so ask yourselves the question "is that the actions of a dishonest man?"

I could go through all of the above to explain why they were not relevant, but I am sure that you can appreciate, as a police officer A and B were not applicable, C and D were not relevant,
E was totally irrelevant because I was aware the day earlier, that I was going to be arrested and F was a total non event because I was a police officer, with a family, in a mortgaged home, with a registered vehicle so was I going to go missing? I think not!

Nevertheless here I was being 'processed' and totally traumatised by the whole experience.

I had requested assistance from a legal representative and the Police Federation had provided them via their solicitors and for that I am so very thankful because without their assistance, I could very well have been 'set up' by the Police!

The solicitor who attended was called Richard and I am eternally grateful to him for his robust professionalism and dedication he showed towards my injustice.

Richard actually spoke to me after the event about how disgusted he was seeing the way in which I was treated and agreed with me about the arrogance displayed by the two female Detective Officers, one of whom was a Detective Sergeant, when they interviewed me.

For any Police investigation, legislation requires that, prior to any interview of a suspect, there must be a 'disclosure process' where the Police inform the solicitor of any evidence they have and this will then allow the interview to progress fairly without things being 'dropped' onto the suspect which would then necessitate a further break in interview for consultation between legal representative and suspect. This also allows the caution to become effective because, should the suspect reply 'no comment' after having had fair and proper disclosure, then the courts can, quite rightly, draw inferences from their silence and could be convicted!

As far as the Detectives investigating me were concerned, they were NOT going to tell Richard, my solicitor, anything whatsoever despite this being a tape recorded disclosure making them look extremely arrogant, and so his advice to me was to make a 'prepared statement' with my whole account concerning the allegations made and then this would be served upon the Detectives at the start of the interview and I was then to make 'no comment' replies unless indicated otherwise by him, which is the correct course of action to take where, in effect, the Police investigators were extremely hostile and most certainly were acting like they were 'judge and jury'.

I did as I was instructed, yet I wanted so much to tell them how nasty, corrupt and vindictive Constable B.B. was but I knew, deep within me, that this would fall on 'deaf ears' and so was pointless!

Throughout the interviews, of which there were several, the Detectives were trying to 'befriend' me and 'put words into my mouth' by putting 'scenarios' forward of how they saw things and invited me to respond, which I did of course, with no comment and this visibly annoyed and frustrated them, but I had done nothing wrong and I was not going to allow their 'career development c.v.' to include how they had helped convict a Police Sergeant because I was innocent and a victim of a malicious investigation!

Investigations are subject to legislation which MUST BE FOLLOWED and one aspect of this was 'The Criminal Procedure and Investigations Act 1996' which they blatantly IGNORED throughout, despite my insistence on tape, that they must follow up my witnesses to prove my innocence.

Section 22 of the above act places a duty on investigators to pursue ALL REASONABLE lines of enquiry and to RECORD AND RETAIN ALL RELEVANT MATERIAL and I had provided NAMES AND ADDRESSES of people who could prove that Constable B.B. was in fact LYING and thus, had the investigation been unbiased, should have led to her arrest and charges of Perverting The Course of Justice, malfesis in public office and several others, but despite their ACCEPTING my information and ASSURING ME IT WOULD BE LOOKED INTO, it was not and, at a later date, when I requested copies of my interview tapes, this was denied to me despite it actually being not only 'good practise', but also MY RIGHT AS A DEATAINED PERSON being investigated for an allegation!

The legislation states under section 22(1) of the above act that a criminal investigation is an investigation conducted by Police Officers with a view to it being ascertained –

i) Whether a person should be charged with an offence,

Or,

ii) Whether a person charged with an offence is guilty of it.

Section 22(2) of the above act states that in this part, references to material are to material of all kinds, and in particular include references to –

i) Information,

And,

ii) Objects of all descriptions.

Section 22(3) states that references to recording information are to putting it in a durable or retrievable form (such as writing – statements from MY witnesses, or tape).

Never, in all of my twenty five and a half years service had I felt so disillusioned with the Police than I did after this day and my 'trust' and 'pride' in the 'Organisation' would never return to me, yet my ordeals were not at an end yet!

I was placed upon Police bail for 3 months and every day all I could see was darkness surrounding me, so much so that I contemplated taking my own life and was so close to it one afternoon, that I would have done so had it not been for a family member and their actions.

On this date in question, I had had yet more bad experiences with a Detective Inspector from the Foxtrot on the telephone and, whilst sat in my garden, I was reduced to tears, seeing no way out of this horror and a family member, came and sat with me and saw, quite obviously, that my demeanour and body language was changing and I was, in effect, entering the 'zone' (something that many suicide victims fall into immediately prior to taking action to end their lives from what Coroners Officers have told me) and, although this family member was talking to me and holding my hand, I was oblivious to their presence, only realising consciously that they were there when they shouted at me that I was in fact, crushing their hand with my grip.
Something that I would never do is hurt my family young or old and that brought me back so to speak, but I was still 'not myself' and so they telephoned my wife at work and she came straight home to me.

I still find it hard to write down how close I came on that occasion to ending my life and all my family watched me closely from then on for which I am so thankful of!

EVERY DAY I imagined being imprisoned for something I had NOT done and this traumatised me extremely because I strongly believed that I was losing my battle to prove my innocence and that the Police investigators just wanted a result, the result being my being sent down!

Whilst on Police bail, the investigating Officers attended the work place of Constable B.B. to inform her that it was unlikely (unlikely!! They should have been telling her that there was no evidence to support her malicious allegations, not unlikely!) that a prosecution would occur against me and, as I was reliably informed via the Police Federation, as soon as she heard this, she 'kicked off' with the Detectives accusing THEM of being corrupt and then stormed off saying "this is not right, this is NOT GOING TO PLAN!" and was subsequently instructed to return to her place of work by her Federation Representative, a female Inspector who then attempted to 'calm Constable B.B. down'!

I asked the question, as I am sure you are now, why would a woman who is supposedly telling the truth, shout about things not 'going to plan' and then accuse the investigating Officers of being corrupt in their actions?

The only answer obvious to me, and, believe me, I know, is that this woman was LYING!

The attacks upon me never ceased and, during my time on Police bail, Constable B.B. made further allegations that I was intimidating her as a witness and how was I doing this you may ask?

I was allegedly 'growling' at her through the windscreen of my vehicle if I ever saw her travelling in the opposite direction towards me on 30 mph roads, yet I was never interviewed about this allegation, merely 'warned'!

I insisted that the investigating Officers deal with me for this allegation and, should they feel it 'necessary and proportionate', arrest me for witness intimidation, but they did not, which was a pity because, for four out of the alleged six incidents, I was in company of another adult who would be my witness and proof that Constable B.B. was a liar and I told the investigating Officers of that fact which, I suspect, is why they decided not to proceed with that!

When would my nightmare ever end and, more importantly, when were the 'Organisation' representatives going to realise that I was actually the victim in this whole matter and Constable B.B. was the offender?

Well, it wasn't going to stop for quite some time because, to illustrate just how intent the 'Organisation' were in their 'removing me' from office one way or another, when they submitted their 'file of evidence' to the Crown Prosecution Service or C.P.S. as they are known (basically just a bundle of information as opposed to evidence because evidence can prove guilt and they did not have any), the C.P.S. returned it with their advice that there was no evidence to offer and my matter should be finalised as No Further Action or N.F.A. due to lack of evidence, but no, that was not satisfactory for these individuals and so they sent the same file off to ANOTHER C.P.S. who, not surprisingly, returned with the same advice of N.F.A!

So that should have been it, end of Police bail, return of my mobile phones that had been forensically examined and a little 'piece of mind' for me, shouldn't it?

The Police retained my phones for some time more until I made a complaint to my Federation Rep and threatened to 'go public' with everything because I now felt that if I did go public, I certainly WOULD NOT ensure, as I have with this, that I did not breach any confidentiality or legislation, and I would 'whistle blow' EVERYTHING that I could possibly, having total disregard to any consequences and I told my Rep "If they are so intent on prosecuting me for something that I have NOT done, then I will give them something to prosecute me for that I actually HAVE DONE!"

My Federation Rep, realising the effect that this was now having upon my health and state of mind, made me a promise PROVIDING I made him one and that was that I MUST NOT DO ANYTHING HASTILY and I MUST LET HIM GO TO THE FOXTROT DIVISION TO GET MY PHONES BACK BEFORE I ACT!

Well, obviously, I trusted him with my life, he was such a genuine copper and, although we were the same rank, I could not have respected him more because he was not 'letting go' of my case and, I later found out, was totally disillusioned and disgusted with my treatment by the Organisation which was eventually, after some considerable thought, one of the reasons he retired early because he had lost the 'fire' that drove him after accompanying me through my ordeal as much as he could and he was actually becoming drained and ill as a direct result!

I can understand that completely because, like so many other Federation members who had helped me, he was, together with Richard my solicitor, a 'defensive guardian angel' deflecting as much as could possibly be done!

In recent times of 'modernisation' I have commented on social networking sites to Police Officers that, despite their 'upset' with, in their terminology, the 'failures' of the Police Federation, they should remain members because I do not know what I would have done without the help, support and guidance of the representatives of The Police Federation of England and Wales and cannot thank them enough for their belief in me!

My Federation Rep. was true to his word and, despite being due to finish his tour of duty at 4 pm, he travelled to the Foxtrot Division and demanded to see one of the Detectives who were dealing with me, which he did!

Initially, the Officer claimed that my phones could not be retrieved because they were in the 'property system' and so my Rep. gave them a somewhat 'heated' lecture on the Theft Act 1968 and the fact that, if their investigation was concluded into my phones, which it was, then if they retained them any longer without a lawful reason and refused to return them, which they were doing, then they themselves were committing the offence of Theft and he would be left with no other alternative than to either arrest them or contact their Chief Superintendent to make a 'formal complaint' which could result in their being arrested or at the very least subjected to a discipline investigation!

Not surprisingly, my Federation Rep. returned to my home address several hours after his official finishing time in possession of my mobile phones and I could not thank him enough, but it did illustrate something quite disturbing too and that was that these 'Organisational representatives' were still trying to make my life a misery by delaying actions.

Shortly after this, perhaps a couple of weeks, my Police bail was officially cancelled and, as far as that set of malicious lies were concerned, my name and reputation had been cleared, but I still faced a 'Bullying' internal investigation!

My wife, immediate family, sister and her husband were so supportive and like a 'rock' for me throughout and I will NEVER forget that!

I did, several months after my arrest, attempt to obtain the CCTV record from the Custody Office on the Foxtrot Division with a view to suing the Police but, not surprisingly, the CCTV records had been 'destroyed' and I know why, because it would show, in real time, that my arrest had been unlawful and the Police would not want to be shown as corrupt now, would they?

I did, eventually return to work but I underwent 'hypnotherapy' with my psychiatrist, Dr Dootson to give me the strength I needed to walk through the security gate and doors.

This was not because I was ashamed, I was not, my name and reputation was exonerated and all I faced now, as I understood, was an internal investigation to answer yet more of Constable B.B's false allegations that I was bullying her, no, I needed 'hypnotherapy' because each time I thought of walking into work, in my head I was back on the Foxtrot Division being placed under arrest and the panic attacks that I suffered because of this were horrendous!

I was actually diagnosed by my psychiatrist as suffering from Post Traumatic Stress Disorder (PTSD) which is something that is usually linked to 'life threatening' experiences and experienced some quite graphic and unnerving nightmares following my arrest and disgusting treatment at the hands of the 'organisation'.
Many a night my wife would be woken up by my 'thrashing' around in bed and shouting and swearing about corruption and 'bent cops' and she would attempt to wake me up, which sometimes would work, but on the occasions that it did not, she would quickly get out of bed fearing that I would, in my sleep, become physically more violent and so would try to wake me by shouting my name!

I could never live with myself if I hurt my wife and yet I was not in control of my subconscious and eventually woke up shaking and in a cold sweat, but, more worrying, frightened or extremely angry until the realisation occurred that these were not real and merely nightmares.

I remember the nightmares vividly and to this date, I still suffer nights filled with these regularly!

In my nightmares I was a soldier in Afghanistan or Iraq and my 'bosses' out there were demonic images of the bosses and Officers that I was actually fighting against in the Police.
I would be given orders to go out and fight the 'enemy' but I was given a weapon with no ammunition, no body armour and no 'back up' so, in effect, I was to 'stand alone' in my fight against evil and believe me I had no bloody idea why my nightmares placed me into such war zones and why as a soldier?

Other occasions saw me as a Police Officer but in a life threatening situation such as a serious disturbance, riot, and again I was alone taking 'flak' whilst the bosses and other Police simply looked on and laughed!

I did start to punch out and kick a lot when my nightmares took hold later on and became more frequent, but fortunately, my wife had become 'wise' to the warning signs and simply took to leaving our bed until I awoke.

These experiences troubled me extremely and so I took to discussing them with Dr 'E.E' to try to gain 'control' of them because, in my mind, if I could 'rationalise' them then perhaps they would subside and hopefully disappear!

As I explained my nightmares, Dr 'E.E' listened very acutely and then gave me her professional opinion of the origins of these which, after she had told me and I had taken time to 'digest' her thoughts, it seemed logical that they were closely linked to my personal trauma.

I was a Police Officer fighting against corruption and lies which involved many ranking Officers and my sub conscious saw this as a 'war' if you like, hence the conflict war zones such as Iraq and Afghanistan and I felt helpless because nobody would listen to me apart from the Federation and so my sub conscious put me into scenarios where I was being 'fitted up' (no ammunition, body armour, back up etc) in these war zones!

I respect our Armed Forces and the jobs they do intently and consciously would never put myself onto a parallel with what they do and experience, but we have no control whatsoever on our sub conscious and how it works on us when we are asleep and this is how mine was trying to 'rationalise' and deal with my trauma, so I have to accept that, no matter how uncomfortable and frightening it was.
Later in the book I will explain how I became passionate about 'Help for Heroes', a charity that aims to raise as much money as possible to assist our wounded heroes and their families, but also, sadly, of the attacks that were made upon me whilst raising monies for this and the lack of action taken by the Police Organisation as a whole, but I am sure that does not surprise you by now does it?

I wrote a poem about my personal experience with what, in my opinion, I believed was nothing less than corruption and called it 'A Personal Message From Me' :-

A Police Officer should be trusted,

They should believe in the Truth,

Serve the Crown.

But in my career, I am sorry to say,

There are many who have let that down.

They are concerned for no one but themselves,

Will work to their own agenda,

They will push you away with no more than a glance,

Like a drunk who is out on a 'bender'!

I have, from my own experience,

Seen closing of ranks and lies!

This is not from rumour or 'bush telegraph',

It was seen through my own pair of eyes!

If you do not comply with the hierarchy words,

They will go out to destroy you as if shooting a flock of birds.

In my twenty four years,

I have served Truth and Justice and am proud in my heart of that fact,

But in the past nine years I have been dealt many blows,

Thus, it is now I decided to act!

Let the Truth come out, let the Public know,

What this Organisation can be!

The representatives are nothing more than puppets,

Being controlled by many an M.P!

There are the few, of whom I am one,

Who say enough is enough!

But when I have stood up for what I believe,

I have found that the sea becomes rough!

Corruption, Bullying, Lies and Deceit,

They are so very alive!

And as this stands, right here, right now, Alone I stand to strive!

To strive where others have never dared to tread,

To bring out what is right and true!

But for that task, a heavy price I have paid,

Knocking me down and making me blue!

Like the phoenix, I will rise from the ashes,

To challenge them one and all!

To bring out the truth, no matter what cost,

No matter how many will fall!

For to have been truthful, full of honour and full of pride,

Because I could serve the public and the crown,

I am no longer fearful of reprisals,

I will ensure justice takes the corrupt down!

This may take some time and my energy within,

But the outcome is worth all the pain!

Because to do this right now,

With honesty and truth by my side,

I know that all those decent will gain.

That is you, the members of public,

Good colleagues, their families as well,

To restore what I joined the police for,

To refill the decency well!

CHAPTER SIXTEEN – THE BEGINNING OF THE END.

After the 'storm' so to speak and whilst I was a little 'low' and on sickness leave, I saw on the news that a soldier who had only just been sent to Afghanistan after completing his basic training and 'coming of age' where he could be sent on 'active duty' in a conflict zone, had been returned to the U.K. suffering severe injuries and he was only 19 – 20 years old!

He had only completed six weeks of his first tour of duty when he was injured and lost both legs and an arm as a result of an explosion and I simply began to cry as I heard this news because this brave young soldier was in the same age group as my young family members and it made my mind begin to race about how his mother and father, brother or sister were coping now and how the soldiers life had completely changed from that moment on and WHO would help him from now on in his life?

So, at that precise moment, I knew I had to do something, ANYTHING, to help and, after TWENTY SIX YEARS, decided that I would train to run ANOTHER MARATHON and obtain sponsorship to raise funds as I did all those many years ago when I should have died as a sixteen year old boy!

I wrote a poem dedicated to all our service personnel and I hope that, when you read it, it may inspire you to go that 'extra mile' to support them.

I called it 'Remember the Heroes':-

Remember all the fallen heroes,

Past and present so....

For no longer do we remember those who died in two World Wars, oh no!

We remember recent conflicts,

Those tender brave young lives....

They gave their all and died in action,

To protect all children, husbands and wives!

We should NEVER FORGET, that is what is said,

So please remember them when you lie safe in your bed.

For no longer do they breathe or live,

Like sand, they've passed through life's' grave sieve.

The families they leave are left to cry,

For their special people, they did die!

Help all the Heroes that have fought for us all...

Give them RESPECT,

Give them LOVE,

So that they can feel PROUD and feel TALL!

God bless our Heroes.

In addition to that, I wanted to do something more 'immediate' because training for a marathon was not something that could be done overnight and so I contacted Help for Heroes and obtained collection boxes, banners, wrist bands and other items that could be exchanged for a donation to the charity and then spent several weeks organising a permit from the local council to allow me to carry out 'street collections' in FOUR town centres.

This would be the ONLY TIME I would ever wear my TWO MEDALS I had received during my service because, as far as I was concerned, they were of no pride to me, being awarded by what, in my opinion, was a corrupt Organisation that I was now beginning to despise, but if, by wearing them whilst collecting, they aided contributions from the public, then they were of some use but after that, they would go away to collect dust!

It all went well, on one occasion, I was helped by a family member and, over four very cold days in November 2009, I successfully raised £881-00 approximately for the charity!

The down side to this was that on one collection date, no other than Constable B.B. saw me and made every effort to walk past me with her young son and 'snigger' and 'grin' as she went past, not once, but TWICE, because she took it upon herself to walk down the main road and then, when at the bottom, turn around and walk back up, again 'sniggering' and 'grinning' in a 'sly' way before using a crossing right next to where I was collecting, to cross the road!

There was two other crossing points where she could have gone, but no, she wanted to 'snigger' and 'grin' at me because she felt TOTALLY UNTOUCHABLE now and, had I not been the decent human being that I am, I could have acted, but I did not!

This was also witnessed by a family member AND was most definitely covered by CCTV because I was situated right opposite a camera post with FIVE cameras on it and outside a building society entrance which had a camera on!

Instead of acting at that time, I decided that I would make this known to my Inspector, D.I. Vickery when he visited me at my home and inform him that I wished to make a complaint of harassment under the 'Protection from Harassment' Legislation and of the CCTV and family member evidence available now, so this I did, with my wife present and, unsurprisingly, D.I.Vickery stated it would be better to allow my bullying investigation to be concluded before progressing this but that he was aware of my complaint and would move it on further AFTER everything else was over!

Needless to say, HE DID NOT, and despite my making an official complaint about that as well, nothing was ever progressed any further!

In January 2010 I commenced my training to run a local Marathon which was to be held in April that same year and I was intent on successfully completing that and obtaining as much monies as I possibly could, yet even doing this training I was not out of the 'firing line' of Constable B.B. and her lies.

I had made several training routes which consisted of varying distances to enable me to build up my stamina and long distance fitness and one of these consisted of running along a main arterial route which went past the cul-de-sac where Constable B.B. lived!

I saw this individual on numerous occasions but ignored her and her family completely, continuing with my running and all seemed well until, one day when I was back in work, I was 'summonsed' to an empty office by a female Inspector, and, much to my shock and horror, I was informed that Constable B.B. had made an allegation against me (again) that I had come down her cul-de-sac, stood in front of her window and stared right in at her and one of her children causing her to be in fear!

I was very angry about this and contacted my new Federation Rep. and my wife, to attend because I was most certainly NOT accepting this whatsoever and was totally sickened to the core by more lies and deceit.

When my wife and Fed. Rep. came down, I was informed by the female Inspector that she had seen the 'statement' made and was 'satisfied' there was sufficient 'evidence' to serve me a notice warning me, yet, several months later, when I challenged the same Inspector as to exactly what the so called 'evidence' was, she told me she had 'no idea' because she HAD NEVER SEEN THE STATEMENT!

I refused to sign the warning and made enquiries with the local council CCTV operators to locate me on my training run, which they did and this showed that I was NOWHERE NEAR CONSTABLE B.B's address AT THE TIME SHE INSISTED I WAS and, most importantly, I WAS RUNNING THROUGH THE LOCAL TOWN CENTRE AWAY from where I was alleged to be!

Procedures were not adhered to either which was put forward as an objection by my Fed. Rep. because if I was suspected of committing a criminal offence, which again this was, I should have been served a Regulation 15 notice under the Police (Conduct) Regulations 2008 and yet here they were, AGAIN, the Organisation making their own rules and procedures up instead of following THE LAW!

Despite my bringing this to the attention of internal affairs AND my bosses, I was ignored, as was the CCTV recording and they did what they did to suit their own 'hidden agenda', which, by now, was no longer very 'hidden'!

From that date forward, whenever I went on a training run, I had a member of my family following or travelling in front of me in a car and 'watching' from a distance just in case the evil that was Constable B.B. attempted to make up more lies because there was nothing in this world that was going to prevent me from running the marathon to raise money to help our injured services and their families!

On the day of the Marathon I managed to finish it in 4 hours and 48 minutes, but my body had been stretched to its limits and, at one point I honestly felt I was going to collapse but I had already told my wife to promise me that, should I collapse and heaven forbid, die running this marathon (as has happened to other, fitter athletes more recently), that she must collect the sponsorship from any of those willing to honour their 'pledge' because I was not doing this for me, I was doing it for our brave Armed Forces!

I had a blister 4 inches long and 2.5 inches wide on my foot and could not walk properly for over a week as a direct result, but, by running, I had raised over £1300 for Help for Heroes and so, in total with the street collections as well, that was, with 'gift aid', in excess of £2,500 for such a worthy cause despite the efforts of Constable B.B. to stop me.

So throughout my career I had fought many a battle to protect the public and, most recently, to protect my family and I, yet now, although I was still being subjected to bias and oppression, it was the turn of my Federation Rep. who had only recently taken up my case from the previous Sgt who had taken early retirement because the toll was getting too much for them, something which I respected and understood completely!

My new Federation Rep, on some occasions, was a little 'delayed' in contacting me when I called for help, but he did know his stuff and, when he got his teeth into something, he would not let go, a character trait that was good but also bad because this eventually put him in the 'sights' of other senior Officers and this he told me himself which I will explain later.

I will return back to the 'bullying and harassment' investigation that I was subjected to.
My new Fed. Rep. was present throughout this with me and had to 'object' on several occasions to the 'closed mind' of the female civilian H.R. manager because, again, I was being seen to be 'guilty' before any investigations had taken place, something that I was becoming used to by now, but my Rep. was not and so, quite rightly, raised concerns!

The outcome of the investigation they termed as 'six of one and half a dozen of the other' which basically was a 'sit on the fence' type of result, blame not being placed solely upon any individual and, under normal circumstances, I could accept that as a final outcome because, to be

honest with you, I was, by now, extremely tired of all the accusations I had faced and fought and the investigations I had been subjected to, however, as a nice little 'slap to the face' and purely based on the fact that I had stated I was concerned about what else this woman (B.B.) was capable of, the 'investigators' recommended the following, which is a direct lift from my copy of the document :-
"Of great concern to Sgt Spence has been his fear of what else PC (B.B.) is 'capable of' given his arrest and interview by staff from the Foxtrot Division.
We therefore feel that the Division has a duty of care towards Sgt Spence in this respect and strongly recommend his relocation to another place of work so as not to be working on the same Division as P.C. (B.B.) to help allay his fears".

My concerns were about what Constable B.B. was capable of, not in work, but at any other time towards my family so how would the above provide a 'duty of care' toward me that covers that aspect?

It was yet again, another 'set up'!

Needless to say, the medical experts intervened on this and I remained where I was, much to the annoyance of Division and, from what I had been told, Constable B.B, but I would not 'roll over' and submit to such stupidity like this, ever!

Now, finally, after all the lies, deceit and rubbish that accompanied that, MY GRIEVANCE was about to be heard, in a manner of fashion and my Fed. Rep. was with me every step of the way, as was my voice recorder for 'meetings' about it.

I had three 'meetings' to discuss this, each recorded by me and the 'organisational representative' was a Superintendent who I discovered, from enquiries made, was a 'yes' boss, a 'puppet' and also someone who was interested only in progressing their own career, a trend that was becoming the 'norm' where I was concerned!

Anyway, on the second meeting I put this Supt. in a corner and asked them to make enquiries into whether or not Constable B.B. had been 'gloating' about the result of the bullying and harassment investigation because I had, unbeknown to them, printed copies of such in my possession after I had been 'tipped off' by a good friend and so my 'trap' if you like, was to illustrate how Constable B.B. would lie to a Superintendent as she had to all other ranking Officers previously.

So the meeting was concluded, a date for the next one fixed and I waited, merely waited, because I KNEW I could show what lengths she would go to and perhaps, just perhaps, they would then change their 'tact' and believe me for once!

The date of the next meeting came, the Supt. was there as was my Fed. Rep. In full knowledge of my proof and we commenced!

The EXACT print of Constable B.B. and her 'status' on a well known social networking site ON THE EXACT DATE of the results being given to both of us regarding her bullying allegation was "(B.B.) has had a great week with a long awaited excellent result on Tuesday and a holiday booked for Disney, next year, birthday drinks with friends today, can't ask for more, happy days ☺ xx".

I had this at the ready in my possession and, when the Supt. had finished their usual negative outcome, I asked had they challenged Constable B.B. as I had requested, to which they confirmed that they had and that Constable B.B. had TOTALLY DENIED anything of the sort!

So now it was my turn, all on voice recorder, to inform the Supt. that I had in my possession, a copy of said 'status' with the date and EVERYTHING needed to prove what I was alleging and I particularly brought to their attention that they had, like so many other ranking Officers previously, been manipulated by a LIAR!

I read the exact quote and even offered the Supt. a copy that they could retain and challenge Constable B.B. over because it proved that she would even LIE TO A SUPERINTENDENT, totally disregarding the fact that she, (B.B.) was a Police Officer who should TELL THE TRUTH, the whole Truth and Nothing but The TRUTH!

The Superintendent TOTALLY DISREGARDED THIS PROOF, perhaps because they were embarrassed that I, a meagre Sgt, had shown them to be INCOMPETENT.

At this point I was extremely angry with the Supt. and made it known because, to be quite honest, I had now totally had enough, it was like the 'Organisation' was covering up corruption AND protecting corrupt Officers of varying ranks and my Fed. Rep. had to 'pull my reins in' somewhat before I 'crossed a line' that could see me being sacked or, at best, demoted from my rank and so I was extremely glad he was present and protecting me because he then made my arguments known before the matter was again concluded for a further meeting to be arranged.

This last act by my Fed. Rep. I believe, was the one that made him a target now and, several weeks after this he contacted me, somewhat alarmed, and asked me if I had 'heard anything about him'!

I was taken aback by this question and so I asked my Fed. Rep. to elaborate on this unusual statement and then it ALL came out in the wash!

He had been reliably informed that the 'organisation' was 'after him' because, and purely because, HE HAD FOUGHT MY CORNER and that they were now going 'all guns blazing' to 'take both of us out of the equation'!

Now I was extremely concerned, yet angry and frustrated because, having a Federation Representative telling me this, IT WAS FRIGHTENING.

The question that was now recurring in my mind was, "I've been to hell and back and believed this may be all coming to an end, but what I am hearing now is that they are going to take both of us down AT ALL COSTS so what the hell do I do?"

The advice I received, although not to my liking, was to carry on with my head down and hopefully the dust would settle, but that was just not me, not what I was or am about and I just knew, in my heart, that my days in the office of Police Sergeant, were sadly reaching the end!

I made myself a promise in the coming days that, in one way or another, I would make my plight and the matters and Officers of varying ranks that, in my opinion, were corrupt, known and wrote a poem after reading my horoscopes for that time which I have written below:-

My horoscope was extremely relevant and said the following,

"Curb the urge to do anything radical or drastic.

You thrive in a competitive atmosphere but you also need to realise the best times to make a move and when it might be to your advantage to hold back.

Competition will bring out the best in you.

Whilst other people are strutting around like peacocks convinced no one can beat them, you will quietly and efficiently get on with what you have to do to prove them wrong".

I wrote my poem almost immediately after reading this and called it "Truth and Justice"!

The Phoenix rose from out of a flame,

Flying higher and ready for the fight that's the same!

All past trials and tribulations remembered so much,

But its soul was much stronger,

Beware those who touch!

For the Truth and Justice must always prevail,

And Corruption and Lies has but one path, to fail!

CHAPTER SEVENTEEN – MY FINAL DAYS.

I did as I was asked by the Police Federation and continued my duties to the high standards that I had always done, but during that time, became a victim of crime myself, I had personal property stolen but the most shocking fact of this was that my personal property was actually stolen from WITHIN THE POLICE STATION, INSIDE MY OFFICE!

So this is quite a relevant scenario really because I had been, after all, the victim of quite harsh and arrogant treatment in the latter years of my career and now, there was a thief within, a member of civilian staff or a Police Officer!

I ensured that my crime was reported and that nobody whatsoever, no matter what rank they held, was going to attempt to 'write it off' as lost property or my mistaken belief and the colleagues and friends within the organisation who I trusted, were extremely angry, saddened and full of utter disbelief that somebody, somewhere, could stoop so low and bring their own reputation into disrepute and attack the Sergeant that they respected so much, in such a personal way because the items stolen were not of much monetary value, but of priceless sentimental value and had been bought for me by family and friends when I was extremely low, in an attempt to 'lift my spirits' and put the smile that they all loved so much, back on my face!

I can truthfully say that, looking back on my whole trauma suffered, this was one of the most hurtful and nasty things to be done to me and something that I will never forget.

I was extremely angry and did, in fact, have to be 'pulled to one side' by several trustworthy Constables and spoken to by them because, had they not done so, If I had found the person or persons responsible, irrespective of what rank they held, I would have probably been arrested for the resulting action that I would have taken and that was never in my nature but I was now, for want of a better way to describe myself, completely and utterly 'on the edge' and no longer thinking in a rational way!

I can see that now, looking back, but at that particular moment in my life, the 'kid gloves' had been taken off and this had become 'personal', after all, what was next, my home, my family?

Each day now became harder for me to walk through the office doors and I can relate to what one Constable has recently described to the Police Federation "I love the job that I do, but each morning I awake in a cold sweat and crying at the thought of entering what is now like a pressure cooker"!
That is exactly how I felt then and obviously, from the above, nothing seems to have changed at all.

I was now in a process of 'ill health' retirement, something that I never wanted to be in because, it would mean that I was leaving the career/destiny that I had set my heart and mind on from being the age of eleven, some four and a half years earlier than I should and that, in itself, was upsetting for me because I felt as though I had failed.......failed the public, failed my family, failed my friends and, most importantly, failed myself, but the process was ongoing and, deep down, I knew that this was best for my family, whom had suffered so much along the way with me, more than I really because they had seen me change, suffer, hurt, destroy myself in many different ways and they felt so helpless because what could they do other than to be beside me on that horrific journey and try to 'pick me up' when I fell and provide a 'shoulder to cry on' when I was in such 'dark' places, something that I will be eternally grateful to them for and something that I will never be able to repay fully!

As the time passed, my psychological health began to suffer more and each day filled me with anger about the way things had been, how I had been treated and how it had changed me so much.

I was now taking an increased amount of prescribed anti depressants just to cope and felt as though I just could not breathe anymore!

I was communicating less with people and knew something had to change very soon because, with every step of the ill health process, I was having meetings and evaluations with specialist Doctors and had to 'open doors' that, with expert help, I had closed hopefully never to open again but, because the Police Organisation still did not really want to allow me this 'exit' and would have preferred to have been able to dismiss me, the procedure seemed to have been unnecessarily elongated and I honestly did not know how much more I could take.

I remember my final day actually working in a Police Station so vividly and will never forget it because that was the day I suffered a complete nervous breakdown and I will explain to you exactly why because on that day, my career of over 27 years died!

Previously I had had my Federation representative asking if I had heard anything about him and now, on this, my final day effectively, I was visited by him again together with a Federation Inspector and what they told me, I could not believe, although I knew that I could trust them and this was their way of 'saving me' from something that would, in effect, be damned hard to disprove and would, if the Organisation successfully carried out their 'plans', result in at the very least, my immediate sack!

The explanation I got was "Mitchell, you've fought hard for what you believe in, what is right and you've beaten them, you have won, you can hold your head up high but you must go now, believe us, this is for your own good!"
The Federation representative then continued "the powers that be have failed to push you out so they are now gunning for you. We have been told by an Officer of high rank (Chief Inspector or above), who is on our side with this, that others are going to fit you up by planting either drugs or stolen property in your Police locker or desk drawers (for which there are master keys and codes for security purposes), so that they can arrest you and charge you with a criminal offence!"

The Organisation had now sunk to an completely new low and deviousness with actions such as these to destroy me and I knew they could and in my case certainly would, carry this most corrupt act out.

After such a hard, long fight against corruption and lies, not only was I being seriously threatened, but so was my family and security in such an evil way that I could have gone to prison and knew I could not fight to win!

I remember vividly looking at my Federation representative with total despair, tears now flowing down my face and saying "No ,No, No, this can't be right, all I believed in, all I strived to do to protect and this is how I am dealt with, by corruption and Illegal immoral acts ,No ,No ,No!"

I was now sobbing like a child, nose running and I was physically shaking, I was in fact in the early stages of trauma and shock and I knew, deep inside my heart, that I could no longer fight this 'caring organisation', the career that I had chosen at a very tender age, for I was definitely not going to be dishonoured for a crime or crimes that I did not commit.

I could see the empathy in my Federation Representatives eyes and heard them say "You can leave with your head held high Mitchell, you have done nothing wrong and have beaten them by being honest! You must now go because if you do not, then we cannot help you anymore, it will be out of our capabilities .please listen to us, you MUST GO whilst you still can!"

<u>That was the day I left the Police station for the very last time and never returned!</u>

I was given a lift home by one Federation rep and because I was in no fit state to drive ,the other brought my car home.

Eventually, it was recommended that, due to my treatment by those in power, I could no longer be a Police Officer or in fact, ever work for the Police Organisation again and that I should now be retired under ill health regulations!

Several months after this recommendation, after approval by the Police Authority, I was allowed to go.

I received an 'invitation', not once, but twice, to attend a 'presentation with the Chief Constable where I would receive my 'certificate of service' and discuss my future plans after, what they described would be, a major life changing experience upon leaving the 'Police Family'!

Needless to say, I refused that offer because I never wanted to have any involvement with what I can only describe as, in my own opinion, a corrupt, disloyal and oppressive Organisation and, had I attended, then my dealings with the Chief Constable would not have been to their liking whatsoever.

As recognition of my service to the Crown, apart from my Queens Jubilee medal and long service medal upon which they engraved my name with incorrect spelling, I received a coloured certificate that said what rank I finished as and something along the lines of "In recognition of 25 years service"!

What a beautiful(said with much sarcasm) token of my service.

I still suffer daily as a result of being a Police Officer and, only the other day, when a colleague whom I had supervised was being laid to rest after passing away within three and a half years of retiring and aged fifty two, I went to the church but could not push myself to go in because there were many Police Officers whom I recognised and who had done me no harm but represented the 'Organisation' that was so nasty to me and so I watched from a distance and said my goodbye, in my own private way, to a colleague who was a decent human being.

I will move back to Karma again before I close my book because there is one Constable who seemed to always come up 'smelling of roses', no matter what lies and deceit they said, Constable B.B.
Well, as is commonly believed with 'Karma', what goes around, comes around and it transpires that her husband has finally seen that individual for the evil that she is and has left the matrimonial home and her close family have fallen out with her because, from reliable information, she alleged that he was beating her up, something which could be no further away from the truth, but then that is how she wishes to lead her life, by lies and we all know that, eventually, in one way or another, a liar is eventually found out and then faces justice in whatever form that may take!

KARMA is something we should ALL think about the next time we speak to someone, wouldn't you agree?

I wrote a poem dedicated to my family and friends who were with me throughout.

I called it "A Fresh Start because you're loved".

The darkest clouds have blown away,
The sun it shines for you today!

My life has changed so much, it's true,
But that's because of my love for you!

Through thick and thin, you've all been there,
When all I felt was fear and scare!

I cannot show how much you mean,
You've all made me feel so strong and clean.

I owe my life to all of you,
The love I feel is strong and true!

So please, read this and smile like me,
For Always and Forever, we will be free!

Referring back to my complaints in chapter 13 after I had appealed the initial findings you may wish to know what happened.
Well, it was slowly, very slowly, reinvestigated by the Professional Standards unit of my force but it was paid 'lip service', shall we say. The police only covered the complaints against Constable 'BB', ignoring the other officers of varying ranks that I had brought up despite early on in the initial investigations my querying with them that should a complaint against Police indicate other wrongdoings by more Officers, then would these other Officers be investigated as part of the initial complaint which had now expanded and the answer I was given was "Yes", which is from my own time and experience as a Police Officer, how I recalled it to occur.

The Police even contacted Officers and questioned them about when I was arrested, despite that not being anything to do with my complaint, and I have been totally exonerated regarding that but they were looking, I believe, for anything whatsoever to blemish my character and thus allow them to close the enquiry.

One witness, I am reliably informed by people who still keep me in the loop, was being manipulated by the Investigating Officer to turn everything 'back to front' in an attempt to show me as bad and was also told "You can tell us all about when Mitchell was arrested because, to be perfectly honest with you, these investigations are going nowhere."

'Perfectly Honest', they would not know the meaning of that whatsoever!

I attempted to challenge the Investigating Officer about this, but each time I called she was either 'Out of the office' on enquiries or not yet in from home. Well, me being me, I decided to withhold my number and ring through the main switchboard, ask for the direct extension to be put through to and 'hey presto', the investigating officer answered.

What occurred then was the total denial of any witness manipulation but a slight admission of a conversation with them, Totally 'above board'. Anyway, the slow cogs turned, the outcome was predictable and the final answer was that the Professional Standards Unit did not feel there was anything untoward and closed the matter.

After this, as I have touched upon in a previous chapter, I repealed to the IPCC, which was my right, highlighting many many discrepancies and the fact that no other Officers had been investigated and they responded in the following manner;

As far as other Police Officers and staff were concerned, I should have made separate complaints about them which was in contradiction to what I understood from my time serving and also contradicted the 'Assurances' that the Investigating Officers gave me and so unless I wish to commence the slow process all over again, which had tired my family, then that ended there.

As far as Constable 'BB' was concerned, the complaint as a whole was not referred to the CPS because of the 'Threshold Test' which is something the Police go through before considering processing matters.

Well, I knew it would fail this test if it was the Investigating Officer influencing this because of everything I have covered in this book previously, however, and this is the most important and relevant section for me and, I believe, also for you because it speaks volumes. The IPCC stated the following;

"After reviewing your allegations and the evidence, in my view there IS an indication that a criminal offence may have been committed by Constable 'BB'".

The explanation then went on further saying that standards of proof in a criminal case are extremely high to show that an offence has been committed beyond reasonable doubt compared to those in civil or county courts but this, on its own, in my opinion, illustrated how right I was all along! Unfortunately it doesn't give the justice that should have prevailed not only in relation to Constable 'BB', but towards all the other officers whom, as far as I'm concerned, were corrupt.

<u>I am sure that you, the reader, will make your own decision regarding who was right, who was wrong, who was honest and who was not.</u>

My purpose from the outset has hopefully been successful in giving you the opportunity to read the truth, the whole shocking truth, and nothing but the truth.

After reading my book, you may be asking yourself, "Why did this all happen to me?"

I will answer that very simply...

Because I was an Honest Cop who believed in Protecting Truth and Justice and Fighting Corruption and Lies!

Thank you.

'Mitch'

Printed in Great Britain
by Amazon